T0343690

APPALACHIAN TRAIL

Data Book

2025

APPALACHIAN TRAIL
Data Book
2 0 2 5

Edited by Daniel D. Chazin

MOUNTAINEERS BOOKS is dedicated to the exploration, preservation, and enjoyment of outdoor and wilderness areas.

1001 SW Klickitat Way, Suite 201, Seattle, WA 98134
800-553-4453, www.mountaineersbooks.org

Printed in the United States of America
Forty-seventh edition, 2025

Cover photograph: *Fitzgerald Falls, New York* (Photo by Daniel D. Chazin)

Mountaineers Books titles may be purchased for corporate, educational, or other promotional sales, and our authors are available for a wide range of events. For information on special discounts or booking an author, contact our customer service at 800-553-4453 or mbooks@mountaineersbooks.org.

Printed on FSC®-certified materials

ISBN (paperback): 978-1-68051-801-6

An independent nonprofit publisher since 1960

Contents

Introduction

There are few things more rewarding than hiking the Appalachian Trail, whether you come to it as a novice looking to spend only a couple of hours outdoors or a Trail-tested veteran who has thru-hiked more than once.

This publication provides a ready reference for hikers to the major features of the Appalachian Trail as it winds for more than 2,197 miles from Maine to Georgia. Many hikers find it indispensable to their journeys on the A.T. and save each year's edition with a record of their experiences and accomplishments.

The features listed here include shelters and campsites, road crossings, sources of water, elevations, principal mountain peaks and gaps, and other notable physical landmarks of America's foremost national scenic trail. Locations of areas where lodging, meals, groceries, and post offices are available also are listed, with distances and directions. Additionally, each section is marked with the Trail-maintaining club associated with that segment; club websites are listed on page 93.

The *Data Book* is intended to be useful in broad-scale planning of a trip of any length on the Trail, from home or while on the footpath itself. The *Data Book* does not, however, include sufficient detail for careful, complete planning of a trip. Potential hikers are encouraged to also purchase the official *Appalachian Trail Guide* book-and-maps set for the state(s) they plan to hike or the *Appalachian Trail Thru-Hikers' Companion.* The guidebooks contain detailed descriptions of Trail sections, facilities near the Trail, points of interest off the Trail, background on the history and natural features of the area, and other important information. They each are sold with sets of maps for the state(s) described.

The annual compilation of each edition of the *Data Book* begins with the latest *Appalachian Trail Guides.* The distances and descriptive information are updated to take into account relocations that have occurred since the last edition. That information is supplied to the Appalachian Trail Conservancy by its member clubs and volunteers who help ensure access to the Appalachian Trail experience for all. Each year, more than 4,700 volunteers contribute more than 170,000 hours of work to various projects along the Trail.

The data has been cross-checked by both volunteers and staff members. However, it is impossible to ensure absolute accuracy of the information, and changes may occur during the year of this edition. Trail-enhancing relocations that affect distances between major features are underway in some states; notices of pending relocations are indicated in current Appalachian Trail guidebooks whenever possible. Also, severe weather conditions, fires, and other unpredictable developments might force temporary closings of a section. In September 2024, Hurricane Helene inflicted severe damage on the Trail from Virginia to Georgia, and any closures or detours are not reflected in this year's *Data Book*. Always check www.appalachian trail.org/trail-updates/before you go for the latest Trail information.

To order *Appalachian Trail Guides*, maps, the *Appalachian Trail Thru-Hiker's Companion*, and other ATC publications, go to www.mountaineersbooks.org, or call 800-553-4453. Guides to Maryland/Northern Virginia and Shenandoah National Park can be ordered at www.patc.net. The Pennsylvania guide and maps can be ordered at www.kta-hike.org.

Because maintenance of the Trail is conducted by volunteers and maintaining clubs listed in the appropriate guidebooks, questions about the exact route of the Trail should be addressed to the maintaining clubs or the Appalachian Trail Conservancy (telephone: 304-535-6331; e-mail: info@appalachiantrail.org).

Hikers finding errors or omissions in the *Data Book* are urged to report them by e-mail to info@appalachiantrail.org, or by mail to Data Book Editor, Appalachian Trail Conservancy, P.O. Box 807, Harpers Ferry, WV 25425. Confirmed changes will be included in the next edition.

Safety and Ethics

Being informed and prepared is the best way to ensure your experience on the A.T. is safe and enjoyable. And being a considerate Trail user ensures that the people around you can enjoy their hike and local plants and animals can continue to thrive.

On the Trail, always carefully follow the painted white blazes and directional signs. Other key safety considerations to keep in mind are water, bear safety, and personal safety.

WATER

Regardless of your skill, it is extremely important to plan your hike, especially in places where water is scarce. The Appalachian Trail Conservancy and the various maintaining clubs attempt to locate good sources of water along the Trail but have no control over those sources and cannot, in any sense, be responsible for the quality of the water at any given time. You should ensure the safety of all water you use by purifying water drawn from any source.

FOOD AND BEARS

ATC advocates strongly that backpackers carrying food use an approved food storage container along the entire Appalachian Trail. ATC strongly discourages the use of the "food hang" to secure food. See www.appalachiantrail.org/news/atc-recommends-a-t-visitors-carry-bear-resistant-food-storage-containers.

PERSONAL SAFETY

Although the Appalachian Trail is safer than most places, you should be aware that problems do occur, and a few crimes of violence have occurred during the past five decades. Situational awareness is one of your best lines of defense. Be aware of what you are doing, where you are, to whom you are talking, and trust your gut. Be prudent and cautious without allowing common sense to slip into paranoia. Here are some suggestions:

Use extra caution if hiking alone. If you are by yourself and encounter a stranger who makes you feel uncomfortable, say you are with a group that is behind you. Be creative. If in doubt, move on.

Leave your hiking itinerary and timetable with someone at home. Be sure they know your Trail name, if you have one. Check in regularly, and establish a procedure to follow if you fail to check in. It helps to register your hike at www.atcamp .org, in case a family member needs to reach you during an extended hike. However, *do not broadcast your itinerary or location in real time* on online journals or blogs.

Be wary of strangers. Be friendly, but cautious. Don't tell strangers your plans. Avoid people who act suspiciously, hostile, or intoxicated.

Don't camp near road crossings. You're less exposed to potential negative interactions if you camp deeper in the woods among your fellow hikers.

Leave firearms at home. Although it is now legal to carry (but not discharge) on National Park Service lands and in most other areas with the proper state-by-state permits, firearms could be turned against you, you face a high risk of an accidental shooting, and they are extra weight.

Eliminate opportunities for theft. Don't bring jewelry or other valuables and keep your money hidden. If you must leave your pack, hide it carefully or leave it with someone trustworthy. Don't leave valuables or equipment (especially in sight) in vehicles parked at trailheads.

Use the Trail and shelter registers. Sign in, leave a note, and report any suspicious activities. If someone needs to locate you, or if a serious crime has been committed along the Trail, the first place authorities will look is in the registers.

Report any crime or harassment. Submit a report to the local law-enforcement authorities and ask them to contact the National Park Service 24-hour communications center at (866) 677-6677. You can also let ATC know by sending an e-mail to incident@appalachiantrail.org or calling the information desk at (304) 535-6331.

Report Trail emergencies. For emergencies where you need an immediate response, check the map, guidebook, nearest shelter, or Trailhead facility for local emergency telephone numbers. Leave the Trail at the nearest road crossing and find a telephone or cell phone reception. Know your location and the location of the incident as precisely as possible. Dial "911" or "0" (ask the operator to connect you with the nearest state-police facility) and make your report. Ask the dispatcher to contact the National Park Service 24-hour communications center at (866) 677-6677. Do not use social media for emergencies.

More detailed advice is available at www.appalachiantrail.org/explore/plan-and-prepare/hiking-basics/safety.

LEAVE NO TRACE

The Appalachian Trail Conservancy, in partnership with the Leave No Trace Center for Outdoor Ethics, asks you to help take care of the Appalachian Trail and the wild country it passes through. Please do your part by following the seven Leave No Trace® principles of low-impact use while in the backcountry:

1. Plan ahead and prepare.
2. Travel and camp on durable surfaces.
3. Dispose of waste properly.
4. Leave what you find.
5. Minimize campfire impacts.
6. Respect wildlife.
7. Be considerate of other visitors.

More specific ways those principles apply to the Appalachian Trail can be found at www.appalachiantrail.org/Lnt. The continued existence of the Trail depends, in part, on proper use by those who walk on it. Specific care should be taken not to damage the footpath itself, natural features alongside it, or the property of others through littering or other vandalism, improper fires, or use of vehicles. The needs of other users should always be considered, and special regulations must be followed in many areas. Please keep day-hiking groups to 25 people or fewer and overnight groups to no more than 10 people.

Although more than 99 percent of the Appalachian Trail now crosses public land, the remainder is on private or municipal property, thanks to the cooperation and good faith of the landowners. The Conservancy and its member clubs strongly urge all users of the Trail to respect those private lands and the owners' rights as if the lands were their own.

Public lands are, in a sense, the user's own—shared with all other users—so please proceed accordingly, taking care to obey any regulations imposed on use of the Trail in a particular section. For example, camping permits are required before entering Great Smoky Mountains National Park. On many other parts of the Trail, camping is permitted only in designated areas.

Consult the guidebooks and maps and watch for special signs along the Trail.

A NOTE ABOUT SAFETY

Safety is an important concern in all outdoor activities. No guide-book can alert you to every hazard or anticipate the limitations of every reader. Therefore, the descriptions of roads, trails, routes, and natural features in this book are not representations that a particular place or excursion will be safe for your party. When you follow any of the routes described in this book, you assume responsibility for your own safety. Under normal conditions, such excursions require the usual attention to traffic, road and trail conditions, weather, terrain, the capabilities of your party, and other factors. Changes resulting from maintenance work, storms, and trail relocations are constantly occurring on the Appalachian Trail so be sure to consult appalachiantrail.org/trail-updates before you go. Always check for current conditions, obey posted private property signs, and avoid confrontations with property owners or managers. Keeping informed on current conditions and exercising common sense are the keys to a safe, enjoyable outing.

—*Mountaineers Books*

How to Use the *Data Book*

The *Data Book* is divided into twelve chapters, beginning with Maine at Katahdin and ending with the Approach Trail to Springer Mountain in Georgia. With one exception, each chapter corresponds to a volume in the current series of *Appalachian Trail Guides*. The section beginning on page 34, for example, matches the third volume in the guidebook series, which covers the Trail in Massachusetts–Connecticut. The exception is the Trail route through the Great Smoky Mountains of Tennessee and North Carolina, which is covered in both the Tennessee–North Carolina and North Carolina–Georgia guidebooks. It is included here only in the Tennessee–North Carolina chapter. Other information is listed as follows:

Trail-maintaining clubs are listed in the outside margins next to the section(s) of Trail that each club maintains. The beginning and ending points of each club's range are indicated by a small gray rectangle. Website information for the clubs may be found on page 93.

Trail sections, as numbered and identified in the corresponding guide, are given in the columns to the left on each page, under the heading GBS (guidebook section). Sections are numbered consecutively, from north to south, within each state.

In the right column, under the **Map** heading, the number of the map that covers the area is listed. For more detail about a particular feature or section of the Trail, consult the relevant guidebook section or map.

Distance from north to south is noted for each landmark (Feature). The number is the distance, in miles, of the feature from the northern end of the part of the Trail covered in that specific chapter (read down). The number to the right of the Features and Facilities columns is the feature's distance from the **southern** end of the part of the Trail covered by this chapter (read up). The starting point for the cumulative distance is given at the top of the column.

0.0	Katahdin (Baxter Peak) (5,268')		282.0
1.0	Thoreau Spring	W	281.0

Sometimes the Trail follows a road, ridgeline, lake, creek, or other physical feature for some distance. In those cases, usually only one distance is listed. For roads, this is generally the point at which the Trail first reaches the road proceeding from north to south, or, in some cases, the point representing the end of the section. For ridgelines, this is the highest point. Again, for more complete information about a particular feature, please consult the guidebooks, maps, or both.

Features include significant landmarks, roads, shelters, and other notable locations. Each section contains a list of features along or near the Trail. Towns with post offices (P.O.) are printed in boldface and carry their ZIP Code in the listing. (i.e. **Greenwood Lake, NY, P.O. 10925**) Towns without post offices or with a post office that is far away from the Trail are listed only if the Trail goes directly through them; "P.O." is omitted in those cases.

The **elevations** of selected points along the Trail follow the name of the feature. [i.e. Rainbow Ledges (1,517′)] Those elevations are intended to represent the most significant points in terms of elevation gain and loss and provide the hiker with a general sense of the elevation change along each section of the hike. Of course, many ups and downs have not been referenced in this book, and the difficulty of the terrain may vary considerably. Hikers should use the elevations provided only as a general guide.

Also in the Features column are distances and compass direction to facilities located farther than 0.1 mile from the Trail. See more information about facilities below.

To the right of the list of features, **facilities,** if any, are noted with a one-letter code. In general, all facilities within five miles of the Trail by road are included, unless similar facilities are located closer to the footpath or a facility's inclusion would not significantly benefit the hiker. In some cases, where a specific facility is not available for a great distance, we have included facilities that are more than five miles from the Trail but still within 12 miles.

Shelters, campsites, and water sources are located within about 500 feet of the Trail unless a distance is listed in the Features column. Distances to all other facilities are always noted in the Features column.

CODES

C   *Campsites and campgrounds.* For New Hampshire, the "C" code is also used to indicate those shelters at which tent camping also is permitted.

E   *"East,"* used to designate direction to facilities that are to the right of the Trail when traveling north (i.e., toward Katahdin).

G	*Groceries, supplies.*
L	*Lodgings other than Trail shelters, campsites, and campgrounds,* such as motels, hotels, cottages, and hostels. This code is also used for the Appalachian Mountain Club (AMC) huts in New Hampshire and camps (commercial cottages) in Maine.
m	*Miles.*
M	*Meals; restaurants.*
nw	*No potable water.* This is used in shelter and campsite listings only.
P.O.	*Post office.* Towns without post offices or that are far away from the Trail are listed only if the Trail goes directly through them; "P.O." is omitted in those cases.
R	*Road access.* Only roads open to the public and passable by ordinary automobiles are designated. Included are road crossings and locations where the Trail runs along a road or is adjacent to a road that provides access to the Trail. Where the road crossings are frequent (every two miles or less), lesser ones are omitted.
S	*Shelter.* A three-sided structure, with or without bunks or floors, intended as overnight housing for hikers (also known as lean-tos in some areas). Included in this category are unlocked cabins or lodges, found primarily in New Hampshire, Vermont, Pennsylvania, and Maryland. (See also "L".)
W	*"West,"* used to designate direction to facilities that are to the left of the Trail when traveling north (i.e., toward Katahdin).
w	*Water* (from springs, streams, etc.). In general, where available, water sources are listed about every three to four miles. Other water sources do exist, and not every water source is listed in the Data Book. **Note:** *All water should be purified before use.*
★	Indicates an **Appalachian Trail Community™,** a town designated by the ATC as a participant in A.T. protection work through local education initiatives and land-conservation activity, while ATC helps it with "green tourism" development. A list of designated towns and counties can be found on page 93.

Whether you're planning to hike the A.T. for a day, a week, or for the entire length of the Trail, be prepared with current Trail information, appropriate equipment, and solid outdoor skills—and enjoy your hike!

Appalachian Trail Distances

These sections and Trail points correspond to the beginning and endings of chapters in this book and the eleven-volume series of official Appalachian Trail guides, published by the Appalachian Trail Conservancy.

LENGTH BY SECTION

Maine	282.0
New Hampshire–Vermont	311.7
Massachusetts–Connecticut	142.4
New York–New Jersey	163.7
Pennsylvania	230.0
Maryland–West Virginia–Northern Virginia	95.2
Shenandoah National Park	107.8
Central Virginia	226.8
Southwest Virginia	166.8
Tennessee–North Carolina	304.0
North Carolina–Georgia	167.0

CUMULATIVE DISTANCES

Miles from Kahtadin		*Miles from Springer Mountain*
0.0	Baxter Peak, Katahdin, ME	2,197.4
282.0	Maine–New Hampshire line	1,915.4
593.7	Vermont–Massachusetts line	1,603.7
736.1	Connecticut–New York line	1,461.3
899.8	New Jersey–Pennsylvania line	1,297.6
1,129.8	Pennsylvania–Maryland line	1,067.6
1,225.0	Front Royal, VA	9,72.4
1,332.8	Rockfish Gap, VA	864.6
1,559.6	New River, VA	637.8
1,726.4	Damascus, VA	471.0
2,030.4	Fontana Dam, NC	167.0
2,197.4	Springer Mountain, GA	0.0

Maine

Club	GBS	N to S	Features	Facilities (see page 14 for codes)	S to N	Map
		Miles from Katahdin			*Miles from ME–NH Line*	
		0.0	Katahdin (*K'taadn*) (Baxter Peak) (5,268')		282.0	
		1.0	Abol Trail, Thoreau Spring	w	281.0	
		4.0	Katahdin Stream Falls	w	278.0	
		5.2	Katahdin Stream Campground, Birches Campsite (1,070') (C,S,w on A.T.)	CSw	276.8	
		5.3	Cross Tote Road	R	276.7	
		7.5	Daicey Pond Campground Road (L,w 0.1m E)	RLw	274.5	
		8.8	Big Niagara Falls	w	273.2	
		9.6	Upper Fork Nesowadnehunk Stream (ford)	w	272.4	
		10.5	Lower Fork Nesowadnehunk Stream (ford)	w	271.5	
		11.0	Pine Point	w	271.0	
		14.0	Katahdin Stream	w	268.0	
		14.4	Abol Stream, Baxter Park Boundary		267.6	
		15.1	Abol Bridge over West Branch of Penobscot River (C,G,w on A.T.)	RCGw	266.9	
		18.6	Hurd Brook Lean-to (710')	Sw	263.4	
		21.1	Rainbow Ledges (1,517')		260.9	
		22.9	Rainbow Lake (east end)	w	259.1	
		26.3	Rainbow Spring Campsite	Cw	255.7	
		28.1	Rainbow Lake (west end) Side Trail	w	253.9	
		30.1	Rainbow Stream Lean-to (1,020')	Sw	251.9	
		32.5	Pollywog Stream (682')	w	249.5	
		33.9	Crescent Pond (west end)	w	248.1	
		36.3	Nesuntabunt Mountain (1,520')		245.7	
		38.2	Wadleigh Stream Lean-to	Sw	243.8	
		40.8	Nahmakanta Lake (south end) (650')	Rw	241.2	
		42.3	Tumbledown Dick Trail		239.7	

*Club column (vertical):* Maine A.T. Club

*GBS column (vertical):* Baxter State Park & 100-Mile Wilderness Section

*Map column (vertical):* Maine Map 1

Maine

		Miles from Katahdin			Miles from ME–NH Line	
		43.8	Nahmakanta Stream Lean-to	Sw	238.2	
		45.8	Logging Road			
			(C 1m E)	C	236.2	
		47.7	Pemadumcook Lake (southwest shore)	w	234.3	
		48.3	Potaywadjo Spring Lean-to (710')	Sw	233.7	
		50.1	Sand Beach, Lower Jo-Mary Lake	w	231.9	
		51.8	Antlers Campsite (500')	Cw	230.2	
		53.1	Mud Pond (outlet)	w	228.9	
		56.0	Jo-Mary Road	Rw	226.0	
		59.7	Cooper Brook Falls Lean-to (880')	Sw	222.3	
		62.0	Crawford Pond (outlet)	w	220.0	
		62.9	Johnston Pond Road	R	219.1	
		64.3	Little Boardman Mountain (2,017')		217.7	
		65.6	Spring	w	216.4	
		65.9	Mountain View Pond (outlet)	w	216.1	
		67.5	East Branch of Pleasant River (ford)	w	214.5	
		67.8	East Branch Lean-to (1,225')	Sw	214.2	
		69.4	Logan Brook Road			
			(L,M 4m W)	LM	212.6	
		71.4	Logan Brook Lean-to (2,480')	Sw	210.6	
		72.8	White Cap Mountain (3,650')		209.2	
		73.9	White Brook Trail		208.1	
		74.5	Hay Mountain (3,244')		207.5	
		76.1	West Peak		205.9	
		76.8	Sidney Tappan Campsite (2,425')	Cw	205.2	
		77.7	Gulf Hagas Mountain (2,683')		204.3	
		78.6	Carl A. Newhall Lean-to (1,860')	Sw	203.4	
		82.1	Gulf Hagas Cut-off Trail	w	199.9	
		82.8	Gulf Hagas Trail	w	199.2	

Maine A.T. Club — Baxter State Park & 100-Mile Wilderness Section

Maine Map 2

Maine

Club	GBS	N to S	Features	Facilities	S to N	Map
			Miles from Katahdin		*Miles from ME–NH Line*	
		83.8	The Hermitage (695') (C,w 0.7m E)	Cw	198.2	
		84.1	West Branch of Pleasant River (ford)	w	197.9	
		84.6	Katahdin Iron Works Road	R	197.4	
		85.8	East Chairback Pond Side Trail (1,630') (w 0.2m W)	w	196.2	
		88.0	Chairback Mountain (2,219')		194.0	
		88.5	Chairback Gap Lean-to (1,930')	Sw	193.5	
		88.9	Columbus Mountain (2,325')		193.1	
		90.2	West Chairback Pond Side Trail (1,770')	w	191.8	
		90.8	Third Mountain, Monument Cliff (2,061')		191.2	
		91.3	Third Mountain Trail		190.7	
		95.6	Cloud Pond Lean-to Side Trail (S,w 0.3m E)	Sw	186.4	
		96.5	Barren Mountain (2,670')		185.5	
		99.6	Long Pond Stream Lean-to (940')	Sw	182.4	
		100.4	Long Pond Stream (ford) (620')	w	181.6	
		104.3	Wilson Valley Lean-to (1,045')	Sw	177.7	
		104.7	CPKC Railway		177.3	
		105.0	Big Wilson Stream (ford) (600')	w	177.0	
		107.9	Little Wilson Falls Trail, Little Wilson Stream	w	174.1	
		108.1	Little Wilson Falls		173.9	
		110.9	North Pond (outlet)	w	171.1	
		111.7	Leeman Brook Lean-to (1,060')	Sw	170.3	
		112.8	Lily Pond	w	169.2	
		113.5	Bell Pond	w	168.5	
		114.6	Spectacle Pond (outlet)	w	167.4	
		114.7	Maine 15 (1,215')	R	167.3	
		118.0	**Monson, Maine, P.O. 04464** (900')	★		
			(P.O.,C,G,L,M 2m E)	CGLM	164.0	

Maine A.T. Club

Baxter State Park & 100-Mile Wilderness Section

Maine Map 3

Maine

Club	GBS	N to S	Features	Facilities	S to N	Map
			Miles from Katahdin		*Miles from ME–NH Line*	
		121.0	Shirley–Blanchard Road	R	161.0	
		121.4	East Branch of Piscataquis River (ford)	w	160.6	
		123.7	Horseshoe Canyon Lean-to (870')	Sw	158.3	
		126.8	West Branch of Piscataquis River (ford)	w	155.2	
		130.5	Bald Mountain Pond (outlet) (ford)	w	151.5	
		132.6	Moxie Bald Lean-to (1,220')	Sw	149.4	
		134.7	Moxie Bald Mountain (2,629')		147.3	Maine Map 4
		136.7	Bald Mountain Brook Lean-to (1,300')	Sw	145.3	
		139.5	Moxie Pond (south end) (970')	Rw	142.5	
		144.4	Pleasant Pond Mountain (2,470')		137.6	
		145.7	Pleasant Pond Lean-to (1,320')	Sw	136.3	
		146.1	Boise-Cascade Logging Road	R	135.9	
		148.7	Holly Brook	w	133.3	
Maine A.T. Club	Kennebec Section	151.4	U.S. 201; **Caratunk, Maine, P.O. 04925** (P.O. 0.3m E; C,L,M 2.0m W)	RCLM	130.6	
		151.7	Kennebec River (490') (ferry)	w	130.3	
		155.0	Trail to Harrison's Pierce Pond Camps (L,M 0.3m E; w 0.1m E)	RLMw	127.0	
		155.4	Pierce Pond Lean-to (1,160')	Sw	126.6	
		158.9	North Branch of Carrying Place Stream	w	123.1	
		159.6	Logging Road	R	122.4	
		161.3	East Carry Pond (north end)	w	120.7	Maine Map 5
		162.8	Sandy Stream, Middle Carry Pond (inlet)	w	119.2	
		164.7	West Carry Pond (east side)	w	117.3	
		165.4	West Carry Pond Lean-to (1,340')	Sw	116.6	
		166.1	West Carry Pond (west side)	w	115.9	
		167.2	Roundtop Mountain (1,760')		114.8	
		168.9	Long Falls Dam Road (1,225')	R	113.1	
		170.2	Flagstaff Lake	Cw	111.8	
		171.5	Bog Brook Road, Flagstaff Lake (inlet)	Rw	110.5	

Maine

Club	GBS	N to S	Features	Facilities (see page 14 for codes)	S to N	Map
		Miles from Katahdin			*Miles from ME–NH Line*	
		171.6	East Flagstaff Road	R	110.4	
		173.1	Little Bigelow Lean-to (1,760')	Sw	108.9	
		174.8	Little Bigelow Mountain (east end) (3,010')		107.2	
		178.0	Safford Notch Campsite (2,230') (C,w 0.3m E)	Cw	104.0	
		178.1	Safford Brook Trail		103.9	
		180.0	Bigelow Mountain (Avery Peak) (4,090')		102.0	
		180.4	Avery Memorial Campsite, Bigelow Col, Fire Warden's Trail	Cw	101.6	Maine Map 5
		180.7	Bigelow Mountain (West Peak) (4,145')		101.3	
		182.8	South Horn (3,805')		99.2	
		183.3	Horns Pond Lean-tos (3,160')	CSw	98.7	
		183.5	Horns Pond Trail		98.5	
Maine A.T. Club	High Peaks Section	185.2	Bigelow Range Trail, Cranberry Pond (w 0.2m W)	w	96.8	
		186.5	Cranberry Stream Campsite (1,350')	Cw	95.5	
		187.4	Stratton Brook (1,230')	w	94.6	
		187.6	Stratton Brook Pond Road	R	94.4	
		188.4	Maine 27; **Stratton, Maine, P.O. 04982** (P.O.,G,L,M 5m W; G,M 3m E)	RGLM	93.6	
		193.6	North Crocker Mountain (4,228')		88.4	
		194.6	South Crocker Mountain (4,040')		87.4	
		195.7	Crocker Cirque Campsite Side Trail (2,710') (w on A.T.; C 0.2m E)	Cw	86.3	
		196.7	Caribou Valley Road (2,220')	R	85.3	Maine Map 6
		196.8	South Branch Carrabassett River (ford)	w	85.2	
		199.0	Sugarloaf Mountain Trail		83.0	
		201.1	Spaulding Mountain (4,000')		80.9	
		201.9	Spaulding Mountain Lean-to (3,140')	Sw	80.1	
		203.0	Mt. Abraham Trail		79.0	

Maine

Club	GBS	N to S	Features	Facilities (see page 14 for codes)	S to N	Map
			Miles from Katahdin		*Miles from ME–NH Line*	
		204.1	Lone Mountain (3,280')		77.9	
		207.2	Orbeton Stream (ford) (1,550')	w	74.8	
		209.9	Poplar Ridge Lean-to (2,960')	Sw	72.1	
		210.9	Stream	w	71.1	
		211.3	Saddleback Junior (3,655')		70.7	
	High Peaks Section	212.6	Redington Stream Campsite	Cw	69.4	
		213.3	The Horn (4,040')		68.7	
		214.3	Berry Pickers Trail		67.7	
		214.9	Saddleback Mountain (4,120')		67.1	
		216.9	Eddy Pond	w	65.1	Maine Map 6
		218.8	Piazza Rock Lean-to (2,065')	Sw	63.2	
Maine A.T. Club		220.5	Sandy River (1,595')	w	61.5	
		220.6	Maine 4; **Rangeley, Maine, P.O. 04970** (P.O.,C,G,L,M 9m W)	RCGLM	61.4	
		222.7	South Pond (2,174')	w	59.3	
		225.4	Little Swift River Pond Campsite (2,460')	Cw	56.6	
		230.0	Sabbath Day Pond Lean-to	Sw	52.0	
	Western Maine Section	230.3	Long Pond (2,330')	w	51.7	
		232.1	Moxie Pond	w	49.9	
		233.7	Maine 17; **Oquossoc, Maine, P.O. 04964** (P.O.,G,L,M 11m W)	RGLM	48.3	
		234.5	Bemis Stream (ford) (1,495')	w	47.5	
		238.3	Bemis Mountain Lean-to (2,800')	Sw	43.7	
		240.0	Bemis Range (West Peak) (3,592')		42.0	
		244.2	Old Blue Mountain (3,600')		37.8	Maine Map 7
		247.0	South Arm Road, Black Brook (ford) (1,410'), Black Brook Campsite (G 4.5m W)	RCGw	35.0	
		248.8	Moody Mountain (2,440)		33.2	
		249.7	Sawyer Notch, Sawyer Brook (ford) (1,095')	w	32.3	
		251.1	Hall Mountain Lean-to (2,650')	Sw	30.9	

Maine

Club	GBS	N to S	Features	Facilities (see page 14 for codes)	S to N	Map
		Miles from Katahdin			*Miles from ME–NH Line*	
		252.4	Wyman Mountain (2,945')		29.6	
		255.3	Surplus Pond (outlet)	w	26.7	
		257.1	East B Hill Road (1,485');			
			Andover, Maine, P.O. 04216			
			(P.O.,C,G,L,M 8m E)	RCGLM	24.9	
		257.9	Dunn Notch and Falls	w	24.1	
		261.6	Frye Notch Lean-to (2,280')	Sw	20.4	
		263.4	Baldpate Mountain (East Peak), Grafton Loop Trail (3,810')		18.6	
		264.3	Baldpate Mountain (West Peak) (3,662')		17.7	
		265.1	Baldpate Lean-to (2,660')	Sw	16.9	
		267.4	Grafton Notch, Maine 26 (1,495')	R	14.6	
		268.5	Brook	w	13.5	
		270.9	Old Speck Trail, Grafton Loop Trail (3,985')		11.1	
		272.0	Speck Pond Shelter and Campsite, Speck Pond Trail	CSw	10.0	
		272.9	Mahoosuc Arm (3,770')		9.1	
		274.4	Mahoosuc Notch (east end) (2,150')	w	7.6	
		275.4	Mahoosuc Notch (west end), Notch Trail	w	6.6	
		276.6	Fulling Mill Mountain (South Peak) (3,395')		5.4	
		276.9	Full Goose Shelter and Campsite	CSw	5.1	
		277.9	Goose Eye Mountain (North Peak)		4.1	
		279.2	Goose Eye Mountain (East Peak) (3,790')		2.8	
		279.3	Wright Trail		2.7	
		279.6	Goose Eye Trail		2.4	
		281.0	Mt. Carlo (3,565')		1.0	
		281.4	Carlo Col Trail, Carlo Col Shelter and Campsite (C,S,w 0.3m W)	CSw	0.6	
		282.0	Maine–New Hampshire Line (2,972')		0.0	

Left margin (vertical): Maine A.T. Club · Appalachian Mountain Club · Western Maine Section

Right margin (vertical): Maine Map 7

Club	GBS	N to S	Features	Facilities (see page 14 for codes)	S to N	Map

Miles from ME-NH line

Miles from VT-MA line

	N to S	Features	Facilities	S to N
	0.0	Maine–New Hampshire Line (2,972')		311.7
	1.9	Mt. Success (3,565')		309.8
	4.7	Gentian Pond Shelter/Campsite (2,166')	CSw	307.0
	5.4	Moss Pond	w	306.3
	6.9	Dream Lake	w	304.8
	9.6	Trident Col Tentsite (2,020')	Cw	302.1
	10.7	Cascade Mountain (2,631')		301.0
	15.0	Brook	w	296.7
	16.2	Androscoggin River (750')	R	295.5
	16.5	U.S. 2; **Gorham, N.H., P.O. 03581**	★	
		(w on A.T.; P.O.,G,L,M 3.6m W;		
		C,L,M 1.8m W)	RCGLMw	295.2
	18.4	Rattle River Shelter	Sw	293.3
	22.4	Mt. Moriah (4,049')		289.3
	24.5	Imp Shelter/Campsite (3,250')	CSw	287.2
	27.0	Middle Carter Mountain (4,610')		284.7
	29.1	Zeta Pass (3,890')		282.6
	30.5	Carter Dome (4,832')		281.2
	31.0	Spring	w	280.7
	31.7	Carter Notch, Carter Notch Hut (3,350')		
		(L,M,w 0.2m E)	LMw	280.0
	32.6	Wildcat Mountain, Peak A (4,422')		279.1
	34.6	Wildcat Mountain, Peak D		277.1
	37.6	Pinkham Notch, N.H. 16,		
		Pinkham Notch Camp (2,050')		
		(L,M,w on A.T.)	RLMw	274.1
	39.7	Lowe's Bald Spot (2,860')		272.0
	41.6	West Branch, Peabody River (2,300')	w	270.1
	42.4	Osgood Tentsite	Cw	269.3
	44.9	Mt. Madison (5,366')		266.8

Side labels: N.H Section 1 · N.H Section 2 · N.H Section 3 · Appalachian Mountain Club · N.H.–Vt. Map 1 · N.H.–Vt. Map 2

New Hampshire–Vermont

Miles from ME-NH line   *Miles from VT-MA line*

Club / GBS	N to S	Features	Facilities	S to N	Map
Randolph Mountain Club	45.4	Madison Spring Hut, Valley Way Tentsite (C,w 0.6m W; L,M,w on A.T.)	CLMw	266.3	
	46.3	Thunderstorm Junction, Spur Trail to Crag Camp Cabin, Lowe's Path to Mt. Adams & Gray Knob Cabin (S,w 1.1m W, 1.2m W)	Sw	265.4	
	46.9	Israel Ridge Path to The Perch Shelter (C,S,w 0.9m W)	CSw	264.8	
	47.6	Edmands Col (4,938')		264.1	
N.H. Section 3	51.1	**Mt. Washington, N.H., P.O. 03589** (6,288') (P.O.,M on A.T.)	RM	260.6	N.H.–Vt. Map 2
	52.5	Lakes of the Clouds Hut (5,012') (L,M,w on A.T.)	LMw	259.2	
	53.6	Mt. Franklin		258.1	
	54.2	Spring	w	257.5	
	55.5	Spring	w	256.2	
	56.4	Mt. Pierce (Mt. Clinton)		255.3	
Appalachian Mountain Club	57.2	Mizpah Spring Hut, Nauman Tentsite (3,800') (C,L,M,w on A.T.)	CLMw	254.5	
	58.9	Mt. Jackson		252.8	
	60.3	Mt. Webster (3,910')		251.4	
	63.5	Saco River		248.2	
N.H. Section 4	63.6	Crawford Notch, U.S. 302, Dry River Campground (1,275') (C 1.8m E; M 1m W; C,G,L 3m E; L,M 3.7m W)	RCGLM	248.1	
	66.5	Ethan Pond Shelter/Campsite (2,860')	CSw	245.2	Map 3
	71.3	Zealand Falls Hut (2,630') (L,M,w on A.T.)	LMw	240.4	

New Hampshire–Vermont

Club	GBS	N to S	Features	Facilities (see page 14 for codes)	S to N	Map
		Miles from ME-NH line			*Miles from VT-MA line*	
		72.5	Zeacliff		239.2	
		75.5	Mt. Guyot, Guyot Shelter/Campsite (4,580') (C,S,w 0.8m E)	CSw	236.2	
		77.5	South Twin Mountain, North Twin Spur (4,902')		234.2	
		78.3	Galehead Hut (L,M,w on A.T.)	LMw	233.4	
		81.0	Garfield Ridge Shelter/Campsite (3,900')	CSw	230.7	
		81.4	Mt. Garfield (4,500')		230.3	
		84.9	Mt. Lafayette, Greenleaf Hut (5,260') (L,M 1.1m W; w 0.2m W)	LMw	226.8	
		85.9	Mt. Lincoln		225.8	
		86.6	Little Haystack Mountain		225.1	
		88.7	Liberty Spring Tentsite (3,870')	Cw	223.0	
		91.3	Franconia Notch, U.S. 3, Lafayette Place Campground (1,450'); **North Woodstock, N.H., P.O. 03262** (P.O.,G,L,M 5.8m E; G,L,M 2.2m E; C 2.5m W; L 1.6m E)	RCGLM	220.4	
		94.2	Lonesome Lake Hut (2,760') (L,M,w on A.T.)	LMw	217.5	
		96.1	Kinsman Pond Shelter/Campsite	CSw	215.6	
		96.7	North Kinsman Mountain		215.0	
		97.6	South Kinsman Mountain (4,358')		214.1	
		100.1	Eliza Brook Shelter/Campsite (2,400')	CSw	211.6	
		103.0	Mt. Wolf (East Peak) (3,478')		208.7	
		107.6	Kinsman Notch, N.H. 112 (1,870')	R	204.1	
		109.1	Beaver Brook Shelter (3,750')	Sw	202.6	
		111.4	Mt. Moosilauke (4,802')		200.3	
		116.0	Jeffers Brook Shelter (1,350')	Sw	195.7	

Sidebar labels: Appalachian Mountain Club · N.H. Section 4 · N.H Section 5 · DOC · N.H.–Vt. Map 3 · Map 4

New Hampshire–Vermont

Club	GBS	N to S	Features	Facilities (see page 14 for codes)	S to N	Map
		Miles from ME-NH line			*Miles from VT-MA line*	
		117.1	N.H. 25 (1,000'); **Glencliff, N.H., P.O. 03238** (P.O.,L 0.5m E)	RL	194.6	
		119.5	Mt. Mist (2,200')		192.2	
		122.0	N.H. 25C (1,550'); **Warren, N.H., P.O. 03279** (w on A.T.; P.O.,G,M 4m E)	RGMw	189.7	
		124.6	Ore Hill	Cw	187.1	
		125.2	Cape Moonshine Road	R	186.5	
		126.8	N.H. 25A (900'); **Wentworth, N.H., P.O. 03282** (P.O.,G,L 4.3m E)	RG	184.9	
		130.1	Side trail to Mt. Cube (North Summit) (2,911')		181.6	
		131.7	Hexacuba Shelter (w on A.T.; S 0.3m E)	Sw	180.0	
		133.1	South Jacob's Brook (1,450')	w	178.6	
		137.0	Firewarden's Cabin (3,230')	Sw	174.7	
		137.1	Smarts Mountain Tentsite	Cw	174.6	
		140.8	Lyme–Dorchester Road	Rw	170.9	
		142.8	Dartmouth Skiway (880'); **Lyme, N.H., P.O. 03768** (P.O.,G,L,M 3.2m W)	RGLM	168.9	
		143.7	Trapper John Shelter (S,w 0.2m W)	Sw	168.0	
		144.2	Holts Ledge (1,930')		167.5	
		146.2	Goose Pond Road (952')	R	165.5	
		147.5	South Fork Hewes Brook	w	164.2	
		149.4	Moose Mountain Shelter	Sw	162.3	
		150.2	Moose Mountain (South Peak) (2,290')		161.5	
		151.8	Mink Brook	w	159.9	

*Left margin labels:* Dartmouth Outing Club — N.H. Section 7, N.H. Section 8, N.H. Section 9

*Right margin labels:* N.H.–Vt. Map 4, N.H.–Vt. Map 5

New Hampshire–Vermont

Club	GBS	N to S	Features	Facilities (see page 14 for codes)	S to N	Map
			Miles from ME-NH line		*Miles from VT-MA line*	
		152.0	Three Mile Road	R	159.7	
		154.5	Etna–Hanover Center Road (845');			
			Etna, N.H., P.O. 03750			
			(P.O. 1.2m E)	R	157.2	
		155.9	Trescott Road	R	155.8	
		158.4	Ledyard Spring			
			(w 0.2m W)	w	153.3	
		158.9	Velvet Rocks Shelter			
			(S 0.2m W)	S	152.8	
		159.7	N.H. 120	R	152.0	
		160.4	Dartmouth College;			
			Hanover, N.H., P.O. 03755	★		
			(P.O.,G,L,M on A.T.)	RGLM	151.3	
		160.9	New Hampshire–Vermont Line,			
			Connecticut River (400')	R	150.8	
		161.9	**Norwich, Vt., P.O. 05055**	★		
			(P.O.,G,L,M 0.3m W)	RGLM	149.8	
		166.2	Happy Hill Shelter/Campsite (1,460')	CSw	145.5	
		168.8	Podunk Brook, Podunk Road	Rw	142.9	
		169.6	Tigertown Road, Podunk Road	R	142.1	
		170.2	Vt. 14, White River (400');			
			Hartford, Vt., P.O. 05047			
			(P.O. 8m E)	Rw	141.5	
		173.5	Joe Ranger Road	R	138.2	
		175.0	Thistle Hill Shelter	Sw	136.7	
		175.3	Thistle Hill (1,800')		136.4	
		177.3	Cloudland Road	R	134.4	
		179.1	Pomfret–South Pomfret Road	Rw	132.6	

Left margin labels: Dartmouth Outing Club — N.H Section 9; Green Mountain Club — Vt. Section 1, Vt. Section 2

Right margin label: N.H.–Vt. Map 5

New Hampshire–Vermont

Club	GBS	N to S	Features	Facilities (see page 14 for codes)	S to N	Map

Miles from ME-NH line (left) — *Miles from VT-MA line* (right)

		N to S	Features	Facilities	S to N	
	Vt. Sec. 2	181.3	Woodstock Stage Road (820'); **South Pomfret, Vt., P.O. 05067** (w on A.T.; P.O.,G 0.9m E)	RGw	130.4	N.H.–Vt. Map 5
		183.5	Vt. 12 (882'); **Woodstock, Vt., P.O. 05091** (P.O.,G,L,M 4.4m E)	RGLM	128.2	
	Vt. Section 3	187.3	Wintturi Shelter (1,900') (S,w 0.2m W)	Sw	124.4	
		189.7	Side trail to The Lookout		122.0	
		192.5	Chateauguay Road	R	119.2	
		197.2	Stony Brook Shelter (1,760')	Sw	114.5	
		201.5	River Road (1,214')	R	110.2	
Green Mountain Club		202.0	Thundering Brook Road	R	109.7	
		203.2	Kent Pond (L,M,w on A.T.)	RLMw	108.5	N.H.–Vt. Map 6
		203.9	Vt. 100, Gifford Woods State Park	RCSw	107.8	
		205.3	Sherburne Pass Trail (2,440')		106.4	
		206.2	Maine Junction; Junction with Long Trail; Tucker-Johnson Shelter (S 0.2m W)	S	105.5	
		207.2	U.S. 4 (1,880'); **Killington, Vt., P.O. 05751** (P.O.,G 2.2m E; L,M 0.9m E)	RGLM	104.5	
	Vt. Section 4	209.1	Churchill Scott Shelter	CSw	102.6	
		211.0	Sherburne Pass Trail, Pico Camp (3,480') (S,w 0.5m E)	Sw	100.7	
		213.5	Cooper Lodge, Killington Peak Trail (3,900') (C,S,w on A.T.; M 0.2m E)	CMSw	98.2	
		217.8	Governor Clement Shelter (1,850')	Sw	93.9	
		219.4	Upper Cold River Road	Rw	92.3	

New Hampshire–Vermont

Club	GBS	N to S	Features	Facilities (see page 14 for codes)	S to N	Map
			Miles from ME-NH line		*Miles from VT-MA line*	
	Vt. Section 4	220.2	Gould Brook (1,480')	w	91.5	
		221.0	Cold River Road (Lower Road)	R	90.7	
		223.0	Lottery Road	R	88.7	
		223.4	Beacon Hill		88.3	
		223.9	Clarendon Shelter	CSw	87.8	
		224.9	Vt. 103 (860');			N.H.–Vt. Map 6
			North Clarendon, Vt., P.O. 05759			
			(P.O. 4.2m W; G 0.8m W)	RG	86.8	
		225.0	Clarendon Gorge, Mill River Suspension Bridge	w	86.7	
Green Mountain Club		227.6	Minerva Hinchey Shelter (1,530')	CSw	84.1	
	Vt. Section 5	231.2	Vt. 140 (1,160');			
			Wallingford, Vt., P.O. 05773			
			(w on A.T.; P.O.,G,L,M 2.7m W; G 3.7m E)	RGLMw	80.5	
		231.3	Sugar Hill Road	R	80.4	
		232.7	Greenwall Shelter (S,w 0.2m E)	Sw	79.0	
		233.2	Trail to White Rocks Cliff (2,400')		78.5	
		237.2	Green Mountain Trail to Homer Stone Brook Trail		74.5	N.H.–Vt. Map 7
		237.4	Spring	w	74.3	
		237.5	Little Rock Pond Shelter and Tenting Area	CSw	74.2	
	Vt. Section 6	239.5	Danby–Landgrove Road (USFS 10), Black Branch (1,500');			
			Danby, Vt., P.O. 05739			
			(P.O.,G,M 3.2m W)	RGM	72.2	
		240.8	Big Branch Shelter	CSw	70.9	
		241.0	Old Job Trail to Old Job Shelter (C,S,w 1.3m E)	CSw	70.7	

New Hampshire–Vermont

Club	GBS	N to S	Features	Facilities	S to N	Map
			Miles from ME-NH line		*Miles from* VT-MA line	
	Vt. Section 6	242.5	Lost Pond Shelter	CSw	69.2	
		244.5	Baker Peak (2,850')		67.2	
		246.5	Griffith Lake (north end)	w	65.2	
		246.7	Griffith Lake Tenting Area	Cw	65.0	
		247.2	Peru Peak Shelter	CSw	64.5	
		248.5	Peru Peak (3,429')		63.2	
		250.2	Styles Peak		61.5	
		251.8	Mad Tom Notch, USFS 21 (2,446'); **Peru, Vt., P.O. 05152** (P.O.,G 4m E; C 2.5m E)	RCGw	59.9	
Green Mountain Club		254.3	Bromley Mountain (3,260')		57.4	N.H.–Vt. Map 7
		255.3	Bromley Shelter	CSw	56.4	
		257.3	Vt. 11 & 30 (1,840'); **Manchester Center, Vt., P.O. 05255** (P.O.,G,L,M 5.8m W; G 2.5m E; L,M 2.1m E)	★ RGLM	54.4	
	Vt. Section 7	259.7	Spruce Peak		52.0	
		260.1	Spruce Peak Shelter	CSw	51.6	
		262.2	Old Rootville Road, Prospect Rock	R	49.5	
		263.1	Branch Pond Trail to William B. Douglas Shelter (S,w 0.5m W)	Sw	48.6	
		265.9	Winhall River	w	45.8	
		267.8	Lye Brook Trail to Stratton Pond Campsites and Shelter (2,555') (w on A.T.; C,w 0.7m W)	CSw	43.9	
		268.0	Stratton Pond Trail	w	43.7	
		271.0	Stratton Mountain (3,936') (G,M 1.7m E)	GM	40.7	

New Hampshire–Vermont

			Miles from ME-NH line		*Miles from* VT-MA line	
		274.8	Stratton–Arlington Road (Kelley Stand Road) (2,230')	Rw	36.9	
		278.4	Story Spring Shelter	CSw	33.3	
		279.3	South Alder Brook	w	32.4	
		283.0	Kid Gore Shelter, Caughnawaga Tentsites	CSw	28.7	
		287.0	Glastenbury Mountain (3,748')		24.7	
		287.3	Goddard Shelter	Sw	24.4	
		289.8	Glastenbury Lookout (2,920')		21.9	
		291.6	Little Pond Lookout (3,060')		20.1	
		294.2	Hell Hollow Brook	w	17.5	
		295.8	Melville Nauheim Shelter	Sw	15.9	
		297.4	City Stream, Vt. 9 (1,360'); **Bennington, Vt., P.O. 05201** (P.O.,G,L,M 5m W; L 2.7m E; G 3.9m W)	★ RGLMw	14.3	
		299.2	Harmon Hill (2,325')		12.5	
		301.7	Congdon Shelter	CSw	10.0	
		305.9	Roaring Branch	w	5.8	
		306.5	Seth Warner Shelter	CSw	5.2	
		308.6	County Road	R	3.1	
		311.3	Brook	w	0.4	
		311.7	Vermont–Massachusetts Line, southern end of Long Trail (2,330')		0.0	

Green Mountain Club — Vt. Section 8 — Vt. Section 9

N.H.–Vt. Map 8

Club	GBS	N to S	Features	Facilities (see page 14 for codes)	S to N	Map

Miles from VT-MA line

Miles from CT-NY line

Club	GBS	N to S	Features	Facilities	S to N	Map
	Mass. Sec. 1	0.0	Vermont–Massachusetts Line, southern end of Long Trail (2,330')		142.4	
		1.3	Pine Cobble Trail		141.1	
		2.3	Sherman Brook Primitive Campsite	Cw	140.1	
		4.1	Mass. 2 (650');			
			North Adams, Mass., P.O. 01247;	★		
			Williamstown, Mass., P.O. 01267			
			(P.O.,G,L,M 2.5m E, 2.9m W; G 2.4m E;			
AMC Western Massachusetts Chapter	Mass. Section 2		M 0.7m E; G,M 0.5m W; L 1.6m W)	RGLM	138.3	Mass.–Conn. Map 1
		5.0	Pattison Road	Rw	137.4	
		7.1	Wilbur Clearing Shelter (2,300') (C,S,w 0.3m W)	CSw	135.3	
		7.2	Notch Road	R	135.2	
		10.4	Mt. Greylock, Summit Road, Bascom Lodge (3,491') (L,M,w on A.T.)	RLMw	132.0	
		10.9	Notch Road, Rockwell Road	R	131.5	
		13.1	Jones Nose Trail		129.3	
		13.7	Mark Noepel Shelter (2,800') (C,S,w 0.2m E)	CSw	128.7	
		14.6	Old Adams Road		127.8	
		17.3	Outlook Avenue	R	125.1	
	Mass. Section 3	18.1	Mass. 8 (1,000');			
			Cheshire, Mass., P.O. 01225	★		
			(G 0.2m W, L 0.8m E)	RGL	124.3	
		18.6	Church Street, School Street (P.O.,C,M, w on A.T)	CRMw	123.8	
		19.8	Cheshire Cobbles		122.6	
		22.3	Gore Pond (2,050')		120.1	

Massachusetts–Connecticut

Club	GBS	N to S	Features	Facilities (see page 14 for codes)	S to N	Map
		Miles from VT-MA line			*Miles from CT-NY line*	
	Mass. Sec. 3	22.7	Crystal Mountain Campsite (C,w 0.2m E)	Cw	119.7	Mass.–Conn. Map 1
		26.4	Gulf Road	R	116.0	
		27.4	Mass. 8, Mass. 9 (1,200'); **Dalton, Mass., P.O. 01226** (M on A.T.; P.O.,G,L,M 0.3m W)	RL	115.0	
	Mass. Section 4	28.0	CSX Railroad		114.4	
		30.1	Grange Hall Road	R	112.3	
		30.4	Kay Wood Shelter (C,S,w 0.2m E)	CSw	112.0	
		33.1	Warner Hill (2,050')		109.3	
		33.8	Blotz Road	R	108.6	
		35.0	Cady Brook	w	107.4	
		37.0	Pittsfield Road (Washington Mountain Road); (G,L 4.6m E; M 1.8m E)	RGLM	105.4	
	Mass. Section 5	38.5	West Branch Road	R	103.9	Mass.–Conn. Map 2
		39.2	October Mountain Shelter (1,950')	CSw	103.2	
		41.0	County Road	R	101.4	
		43.3	Finerty Pond	w	99.1	
		45.1	Becket Mountain (2,180')		97.3	
		45.6	Tyne Road	R	96.8	
		46.4	U.S. 20 (1,400'); **Lee, Mass., P.O. 01238** (P.O.,G,L,M 5m W) (L 0.2m E)	RGLM	96.0	
	Mass. Section 6	46.7	Greenwater Brook	w	95.7	
		46.8	Massachusetts Turnpike		95.6	
		48.0	Upper Goose Pond Cabin (C,S,w 0.5m W)	CSw	94.4	
		48.8	Upper Goose Pond		93.6	
		50.7	Goose Pond Road	R	91.7	

Club column (vertical): AMC Western Massachusetts Chapter

Massachusetts–Connecticut

			Miles from VT-MA line		*Miles from CT-NY line*	
		52.7	Brook	w	89.7	
		53.1	Webster Road (1,800')	R	89.3	
		55.0	Tyringham Main Road (930')	R	87.4	
		56.1	Jerusalem Road	RLw	86.3	
			Tyringham, Mass., P.O. 01264 (P.O., L 0.6m W)			
		58.1	Shaker Campsite	Cw	84.3	
		58.4	Jerusalem Road (Fernside Road) (w 0.2m E)	Rw	84.0	
		61.6	Beartown Mountain Road	Rw	80.8	
		62.2	Mt. Wilcox North Shelter (2,100') (C,S,w 0.3m E)	CSw	80.2	
		63.9	Mt. Wilcox South Shelter	CSw	78.5	
		64.7	The Ledges		77.7	
		65.3	Benedict Pond (C,w 0.5m w)	RCw	77.1	
		66.1	Blue Hill Road (Stony Brook Road)	R	76.3	
		67.3	Mass. 23 (1,000');			
			Great Barrington, Mass., P.O. 01230 (P.O.,G,L,M 4m W)	★ RGLM	75.1	
		68.2	Lake Buel Road (L,M 2.5m W)	RLM	74.2	
		69.3	Ice Gulch, Tom Leonard Shelter (C,S on A.T.; w 0.2m E)	CSw	73.1	
		71.4	East Mountain (1,800')	w	71.0	
		72.8	Home Road	R	69.6	
		74.8	Housatonic River	R	67.6	
		75.7	U.S. 7; **Sheffield, Mass., P.O. 01257** (P.O.,G,L,M 3.3m E; M 1.0m W, 0.8m E)	RGLM	66.7	
		77.5	Sheffield–Egremont Road (700')	R	64.9	

AMC Western Massachusetts Chapter

Mass. Section 7

Mass. Section 8

Mass.–Conn. Map 2

Massachusetts–Connecticut

Club	GBS	N to S	Features	Facilities (see page 14 for codes)	S to N	Map

Miles from VT-MA line

Miles from CT-NY line

		79.3	Mass. 41 (Undermountain Road);			
			South Egremont, Mass., P.O. 01258			
			(P.O.,G,M 1.2m W)	RGM	63.1	
		80.2	Jug End Road (Curtiss Road) (w 0.3m E)	Rw	62.2	
		81.3	Jug End (1,750')		61.1	
		83.0	Elbow Trail		59.4	
		83.6	Glen Brook Shelter	CSw	58.8	
		83.7	The Hemlocks Shelter	Sw	58.7	
		84.1	Guilder Pond Picnic Area	R	58.3	
		84.8	Mt. Everett (2,602')		57.6	
		85.5	Race Brook Falls Trail to Race Brook Campsite			
			(C,w 0.4m E)	Cw	56.9	
		86.4	Mt. Race		56.0	
		88.2	Side trail to Laurel Ridge Campsite	Cw	54.2	
		89.2	Sages Ravine (1,340')	w	53.2	
		89.8	Sages Ravine Campsite	Cw	52.6	
		90.2	Massachusetts–Connecticut Line		52.2	
		90.7	Bear Mountain (2,316')		51.7	
		91.3	Bear Mountain Road		51.1	
		91.5	Riga Junction, Undermountain Trail		50.9	
		92.0	Brassie Brook (South Branch),			
			Brassie Brook Shelter	CSw	50.4	
		92.6	Ball Brook Group Campsite	Cw	49.8	
		93.2	Riga Shelter	CSw	49.2	
		94.0	Lions Head (1,738')		48.4	
		96.2	Conn. 41 (Under Mountain Road);			
			Salisbury, Conn., P.O. 06068			
			(P.O.,G,L,M 0.8m W)	RGLM	46.2	
		96.9	U.S. 44 (700')	R	45.5	
		99.7	Billy's View		42.7	

Vertical labels (left margin): AMC Western Massachusetts Chapter — Mass. 9 — Mass. Section 10; AMC Connecticut Chapter — Conn. Section 1 — Conn. Sec. 2

Vertical label (right margin): Mass.–Conn. Map 3

Massachusetts–Connecticut

Club	GBS	N to S	Features	Facilities (see page 14 for codes)	S to N	Map
			Miles from VT-MA line		*Miles from CT-NY line*	
		100.5	Rand's View		41.9	
		100.6	Side trail to Limestone Spring Shelter (C,S,w 0.5m W)	CSw	41.8	
	Conn. Section 2	101.3	Prospect Mountain (1,475')		41.1	
		103.5	Spring	w	38.9	
		104.6	Housatonic River Road	R	37.8	
		105.0	Housatonic River; **Falls Village, Conn., P.O. 06031** (P.O. 0.5m E)	R	37.4	
		106.8	Mohawk Trail (L,M 0.2m E)	LM	35.6	
AMC Connecticut Chapter		106.9	U.S. 7, Housatonic River (500')	R	35.5	Mass.-Conn. Map 3
		107.5	U.S. 7, Conn. 112	R	34.9	
		107.9	Belter's Campsite	Cw	34.5	
		110.1	Hang Glider View		32.3	
		110.9	Sharon Mountain Campsite	Cw	31.5	
	Conn. Section 3	112.1	Mt. Easter (1,350')		30.3	
		112.4	Mt. Easter Road	R	30.0	
		113.3	Pine Swamp Brook Shelter	CSw	29.1	
		114.4	West Cornwall Road (800'); **West Cornwall, Conn., P.O. 06796** (P.O. 2.2m E)	R	28.0	
		114.5	Carse Brook	w	27.9	
		116.7	Cesar Road, Cesar Brook Campsite	Cw	25.7	
		117.8	Pine Knob Loop Trail		24.6	
		117.9	Hatch Brook	w	24.5	
		119.0	Old Sharon Road	R	23.4	
		119.1	Guinea Brook	w	23.3	
		119.2	Conn. 4; **Cornwall Bridge, Conn., P.O. 06754** (P.O.,G,L 0.9m E)	RGL	23.2	

Massachusetts–Connecticut

Club	GBS	N to S	Features	Facilities (see page 14 for codes)	S to N	Map
			Miles from VT-MA line		*Miles from CT-NY line*	
		120.1	Silver Hill Campsite (1,000')	C(nw)	22.3	
		120.9	River Road, Spring	Rw	21.5	
		122.9	Stony Brook Campsite	Cw	19.5	
		123.3	Stewart Hollow Brook Shelter (400')	CSw	19.1	
		125.6	River Road	R	16.8	
		126.1	St. Johns Ledges		16.3	
		126.8	Caleb's Peak (1,160')		15.6	
		127.5	Skiff Mountain Road	R	14.9	
		130.5	Conn. 341, Schaghticoke Road (350'); **Kent, Conn., P.O. 06757** (P.O.,G,L,M 0.8m E)	RGLM	11.9	
		130.8	Mt. Algo Shelter	CSw	11.6	
		131.8	Thayer Brook	w	10.6	
		133.7	Schaghticoke Mountain Campsite	Cw	8.7	
		135.1	Connecticut–New York Line (1,250')		7.3	
		136.3	Schaghticoke Mountain		6.1	
		138.0	Schaghticoke Road	R	4.4	
		138.7	Side trail to Bulls Bridge Road Parking Area (R 0.2m E; G,M 0.4m E)	RGM	3.7	
		139.3	Stream	w	3.1	
		139.4	Ten Mile River (280')	C(nw)	3.0	
		139.6	Ten Mile River Shelter	S(nw)	2.8	
		140.6	Ten Mile Hill (1,000')		1.8	
		141.7	Conn. 55	R	0.7	
		142.4	Hoyt Road, Connecticut–New York Line (400'); **Wingdale, N.Y., P.O. 12594** (P.O.,G,M 3.3m W; M 1.5m W, 2.3m W)	RGM	0.0	

Vertical labels (left margin): Conn. Section 4 · AMC Connecticut Chapter · Conn. Section 5 (N.Y. Section 1)

Mass.–Conn. Map 4

Miles from CT-NY line

Miles from Delaware Water Gap, PA

Club	GBS	N to S	Features	Facilities	S to N	Map
New York-New Jersey Trail Conference	N.Y. Section 2	0.0	Hoyt Road, Connecticut–New York Line (400'); **Wingdale, N.Y., P.O. 12594** (P.O.,G,M 3.3m W; M 1.5m W)	RGM	163.7	N.Y.-N.J. Map 1
		1.0	Duell Hollow Road	R	162.7	
		1.2	Wiley Shelter	S(nw)	162.5	
		1.6	Leather Hill Road (750')	R	162.1	
		6.7	Hurds Corners Road	R	157.0	
		6.9	N.Y. 22, Metro-North Railroad, Appalachian Trail Railroad Station (480') (G 0.6m E; L 2.6m W; M 2.4m W)	RGLM	156.8	
	N.Y. Section 3	9.3	County 20 (West Dover Road); **Pawling, N.Y., P.O. 12564** (P.O.,G,M 3.1m W; C 3.1m E)	★ RCGM	154.4	
		10.0	Telephone Pioneers Shelter	Sw	153.7	
		10.3	West Mountain (1,200')		153.4	
	N.Y. Section 4	14.5	N.Y. 55 (720'); **Poughquag, N.Y., P.O. 12570** (P.O.,M 3.1m W; G 3.6m W; M 1.5m W; L 2.6m W)	RGLM	149.2	
		14.8	Old Route 55	R	148.9	
		16.7	Depot Hill Road	R	147.0	
		17.8	Morgan Stewart Shelter	Sw	145.9	
		17.9	Mt. Egbert (1,329')		145.8	
		20.3	Stormville Mountain Road, I-84	R	143.4	
	N.Y. Section 5	21.7	N.Y. 52 (800'); **Stormville, N.Y., P.O. 12582** (P.O. 1.7m W; G 2.2m W, 2.4m W; G,M 0.5m E, 2m E)	RGM	142.0	
		23.3	Hosner Mountain Road	R	140.4	

New York–New Jersey

			Miles from CT-NY line	*Miles from Delaware Water Gap, PA*		
		26.5	Taconic State Parkway	R	137.2	
		26.8	Hortontown Road, RPH Shelter (350')	RS(nw)	136.9	
	N.Y. Section 6	28.1	Shenandoah Tenting Area	C(nw)	135.6	
		29.2	Long Hill Road	R	134.5	N.Y.–N.J. Map 1
		29.6	Shenandoah Mountain (1,282')		134.1	
		31.8	Raymond Torrey Memorial Shelter (S 0.6m E)	S	131.9	
		33.8	N.Y. 301, Canopus Lake, Fahnestock State Park (C,w 1m E)	RCw	129.9	
	N.Y. Section 7	35.9	Sunk Mine Road (800')	R	127.8	
		37.5	Dennytown Road	RCw	126.2	
New York–New Jersey Trail Conference		40.2	South Highland Road	R	123.5	
	N.Y. Section 8	41.2	Canopus Hill Road (420')	R	122.5	
		42.9	Old Albany Post Road, Chapman Road	R	120.8	
		43.7	Denning Hill (900')		120.0	
		45.6	Old West Point Road, Graymoor Friary	R	118.1	
	N.Y. Section 9	46.2	U.S. 9, N.Y. 403 (400'); **Peekskill, N.Y., P.O. 10566** (P.O.,G,L,M 4.8m E; M 0.7m E; G on A.T.)	RGLM	117.5	N.Y.–N.J. Map 2
		49.6	South Mountain Pass (Manitou Road)	R	114.1	
		49.8	Hemlock Springs Campsite	Cw	113.9	
		50.8	Camp Smith Trail, Anthony's Nose (700')		112.9	
		51.5	N.Y. 9D	R	112.2	
	N.Y. Section 10	52.2	Bear Mountain Bridge; **Fort Montgomery, N.Y., P.O., 10922** (P.O.,G,L,M, 0.7m W)	RGLM	111.5	
		52.3	Trailside Museum and Zoo (124')		111.4	
		53.0	Bear Mountain Inn, **Bear Mountain, N.Y., P.O. 10911** (P.O. 0.3m E; L,M,w on A.T.)	RLMw	110.7	

New York–New Jersey

		N to S	Features	Facilities	S to N	
		Miles from CT-NY line		*Miles from Delaware Water Gap, PA*		
		54.6	Bear Mountain (1,305')	Rw	109.1	
		57.1	Seven Lakes Drive	R	106.6	
		58.1	West Mountain Shelter			
			(S 1.2m E)	S(nw)	105.6	
		59.3	Anthony Wayne Recreation Area	w	104.4	
		59.5	Palisades Interstate Parkway (500')	R	104.2	
		62.1	Black Mountain (1,160')		101.6	
		63.4	William Brien Memorial Shelter	S(nw)	100.3	
		64.6	Goshen Mountain		99.1	
		65.4	Seven Lakes Drive	R	98.3	
		67.6	Arden Valley Road (1,196')			
			(w 0.3m E)	Rw	96.1	
		68.7	Fingerboard Shelter	S(nw)	95.0	
		69.8	Surebridge Mountain		93.9	
		71.0	Lemon Squeezer		92.7	
		71.5	Island Pond Outlet	w	92.2	
		73.0	Arden Valley Road	R	90.7	
		73.1	New York State Thruway (560')		90.6	
		73.3	N.Y. 17; **Arden, N.Y., P.O. 10910; Southfields, N.Y., P.O. 10975** (P.O. 0.7m W; P.O.,L,M 2.1m E; G 1.8m E, 5.7m E)	RGLM	90.4	
		74.5	Arden Mountain (1,180')		89.2	
		75.1	Orange Turnpike			
			(w 0.5m E)	Rw	88.6	
		75.8	Little Dam Lake		87.9	
		76.5	East Mombasha Road	R	87.2	
		77.3	Buchanan Mountain (1,142')		86.4	
		78.2	West Mombasha Road			
			(G 0.6m W)	RG	85.5	

New York–New Jersey Trail Conference
N.Y. Section 10
N.Y. Section 11
N.Y. Section 12
N.Y.–N.J. Map 2

New York–New Jersey

Club	GBS	N to S	Features	Facilities (see page 14 for codes)	S to N	Map
			Miles from CT-NY line	*Miles from Delaware Water Gap, PA*		
	N.Y. Section 12	79.4	Mombasha High Point (1,280')		84.3	N.Y.-N.J. Map 2
		81.4	Fitzgerald Falls	w	82.3	
		81.7	Lakes Road (680')	R	82.0	
		83.2	Wildcat Shelter	Sw	80.5	
		83.5	Cat Rocks		80.2	
		84.1	Eastern Pinnacles (1,294')		79.6	
	N.Y. Sec. 13	85.3	N.Y. 17A; **Greenwood Lake, N.Y., P.O. 10925** (G 1.6m W; P.O.,G,L,M 2m E; G,L,M 3.5m W)	RGLM	78.4	
		90.9	Prospect Rock (1,433')		72.8	
New York–New Jersey Trail Conference	N.J. Section 1	91.3	State Line Trail, New York–New Jersey Line; **Hewitt, N.J., P.O. 07421** (P.O.,G,M 3.7m E)	GM	72.4	N.Y.-N.J. Map 3
		92.4	Long House Creek		71.3	
		93.5	Long House Road (Brady Road) (G,M 0.7m W)	RGM	70.2	
		94.9	Warwick Turnpike (1,140') (G 1.8m E, 2.7m W; L,M 0.8m W; M 1.5m E)	RGLM	68.8	
		95.4	Wawayanda Shelter (S on A.T.; w 0.4m E)	Sw	68.3	
		95.6	Wawayanda Road	R	68.1	
		96.2	Iron Mountain Road Bridge	R	67.5	
		97.3	Barrett Road; **New Milford, N.Y., P.O. 10959** (P.O.,G 1.8m W)	RG	66.4	
		99.0	Wawayanda Mountain (1,340')		64.7	
	N.J. 2	100.4	N.J. 94 (450'); **Vernon, N.J., P.O. 07462** (P.O.,G,M 2.4m E)	★ RGM	63.3	

New York–New Jersey

Miles from CT-NY line

Miles from Delaware Water Gap, PA

		N to S	Features	Facilities	S to N	
		101.3	Canal Road	R	62.4	
		102.0	Pochuck Creek footbridge		61.7	
		102.7	County 517	R	61.0	
		104.2	County 565;			
			Glenwood, N.J., P.O. 07418			
			(P.O. 0.7m W; L 1m W)	RL	59.5	
		105.4	Pochuck Mountain (800')		58.3	
		106.9	Pochuck Mountain Shelter	S(nw)	56.8	
		107.4	Lake Wallkill Road (Liberty Corners Road)	Rw	56.3	
		109.7	Wallkill River	R	54.0	
		110.7	Oil City Road	R	53.0	
		111.2	N.J. 284 (420')			
			(G 0.4m W)	RG	52.5	
		112.2	Lott Road; **Unionville, N.Y., P.O. 10988**			
			(P.O.,G,M 0.4m W)	RGM	51.5	
		113.1	Unionville Road	R	50.6	
		115.4	Gemmer Road	R	48.3	
		118.0	County 519	R	45.7	
		119.3	High Point Shelter	Sw	44.4	
		119.8	Side trail to High Point Monument		43.9	
		121.0	N.J. 23 (1,500')			
			(w on A.T.; G 2.5m E, 4.3m W;			
			L 1.4m E, 4.4m W; M 4.3m W)	RGLMw	42.7	
		123.9	Trail to Rutherford Shelter			
			(S,w 0.4m E)	Sw	39.8	
		126.3	Deckertown Turnpike	R	37.4	
		126.5	Mashipacong Shelter	S(nw)	37.2	
		129.1	Crigger Road	R	34.6	
		129.9	Sunrise Mountain (1,653')	R	33.8	
		132.3	Trail to Gren Anderson Shelter	Sw	31.4	

Left margin (vertical): New York–New Jersey Trail Conference — N.J. Section 2, N.J. Section 3, N.J. Section 4

Right margin (vertical): N.Y.–N.J. Map 3

New York–New Jersey

		Miles from CT-NY line		Miles from Delaware Water Gap, PA		

New York–New Jersey Trail Conference

N.J. Section 5

		133.4	Culver Fire Tower		30.3	
		135.4	Culvers Gap, U.S. 206 (935');			
			Branchville, N.J., P.O. 07826			
			(P.O. 3.4m E; G on A.T., 1.6m E;			
			L 2.5m E, 1.9m W; M 0.1m W, 0.6m E)	RGLM	28.3	
		139.0	Brink Road Shelter			
			(S,w 0.2m W)	Sw	24.7	
		141.2	Rattlesnake Mountain (1,492')		22.5	
		143.0	Buttermilk Falls Trail		20.7	
		146.0	Blue Mountain Lakes Road	Rw	17.7	
		149.9	Millbrook–Blairstown Road (1,260')	R	13.8	
		150.3	Rattlesnake Spring	w	13.4	
		150.9	Catfish Fire Tower (1,565')		12.8	
		153.3	Camp Mohican Road, Mohican Outdoor Center			
			(C,L,w 0.3m W)	RCLw	10.4	

N.J. Section 6

N.Y.–N.J. Map 4

		157.7	Garvey Springs Trail	w	6.0	
		157.8	Sunfish Pond (1,382')		5.9	
		159.1	Backpacker Site	C(nw)	4.6	
		160.7	Holly Spring Trail			
			(w 0.2m E)	w	3.0	
		162.3	I-80 Overpass	R	1.4	
		162.6	Delaware Water Gap National			
			Recreation Area Information Center	Rw	1.1	
		163.7	Delaware River Bridge (west end),			
			New Jersey–Pennsylvania Line (350')	R	0.0	

Pennsylvania

Club	GBS	N to S	Features	Facilities (see page 14 for codes)	S to N	Map

Miles from
Delware Water Gap, PA

Miles from
PA-MD line

		0.0	Delaware River Bridge (west end), New Jersey–Pennsylvania Line (350')	R	230.0	
		0.2	Pa. 611, **Delaware Water Gap, Pa., P.O. 18327** (P.O.,M 0.1m W; L,M 0.4m W; G,L 3.2m W)	★ RGLM	229.8	
		0.9	Council Rock		229.1	
		1.7	Lookout Rock		228.3	
		2.7	Mt. Minsi (1,461')		227.3	
		4.7	Totts Gap		225.3	
		6.6	Kirkridge Shelter (1,500')	S(nw)	223.4	
		7.2	Fox Gap, Pa. 191	R	222.8	
		8.5	Wolf Rocks Bypass Trail (north end)		221.5	
		8.8	Wolf Rocks		221.2	
		9.3	Wolf Rocks Bypass Trail (south end)		220.7	
		15.7	Pa. 33 (980'); **Wind Gap, Pa., P.O. 18091** (P.O.,G,M 1m E; L 0.1m W)	★ RGLM	214.3	
		16.7	Hahns Lookout		213.3	
		20.3	Leroy A. Smith Shelter (S 0.1m E; w 0.2m E)	Sw	209.7	
		23.8	Smith Gap Road, Point Phillips Road (W 0.6m E)	Rw	206.2	
		26.3	Delps Trail (1,580')		203.7	
		31.1	Little Gap (1,100'); **Danielsville, Pa., P.O. 18038** (P.O.,G,M 1.5m E; w 1.2m W)	RGMw	198.9	
		35.4	Winter Trail (north junction)		194.6	
		36.2	Winter Trail (south junction)		193.8	
		36.4	Pa. 248	R	193.6	

Club/GBS left margin labels (top to bottom): AMC Delaware Valley Chapter — Pa. Section 1; Batona; AMC Delaware Valley Chapter — Pa. Section 2; KTA

Map right margin label: KTA Sections 1–6 Map

Pennsylvania

Club	GBS	N to S	Features	Facilities (see page 14 for codes)	S to N	Map
			Miles from Delware Water Gap, PA	*Miles from PA-MD line*		
	Pa. Section 2	36.6	Lehigh River Bridge (east end), Pa. 873 (380'); **Palmerton, Pa., P.O. 18071** (P.O.,G,L,M 2m W)	RGLM	193.4	
		36.7	Lehigh Gap, Pa. 873; **Slatington, Pa., P.O. 18080** (P.O.,G,L,M 2m E)	RGLM	193.3	
		37.3	George W. Outerbridge Shelter	Sw	192.7	
	Pa. Section 3	42.4	Ashfield Road, Blue Mountain Road Lehigh Furnace Gap (1,320'); **Ashfield, Pa., P.O. 18212** (P.O.,G 2.2m W; w 0.7m E)	RGw	187.6	
		44.8	Bake Oven Knob Shelter	Sw	185.2	
		45.4	Bake Oven Knob (1,560')		184.6	
		45.8	Bake Oven Knob Road	R	184.2	
		47.2	Bear Rocks		182.8	
		47.9	Knife Edge		182.1	
		48.9	New Tripoli Campsite (C,w 0.2m W)	Cw	181.1	
		50.7	Pa. 309, Blue Mountain Summit (1,360') (L,M,w on A.T.)	RLMw	179.3	
	Pa. Section 4	52.9	Fort Franklin Road, Blue Mountain House Road	R	177.1	
		54.8	Allentown Hiking Club Shelter	Sw	175.2	
		56.1	Tri-County Corner (1,560')		173.9	
		62.2	Hawk Mountain Road, Eckville Shelter (600') (S,w 0.2m E)	RSw	167.8	
		67.5	The Pinnacle		162.5	
		67.9	Trail to Blue Rocks Campground (C,G,S 1.5m E)	CGS	162.1	

Club column (vertical): KTA · Blue Mtn. Eagle · Allentown Hiking Club · Blue Mtn. Eagle Climbing Club

Map column (vertical): KTA Sections 1–6 Map

Pennsylvania

Club	GBS	N to S	Features	Facilities (see page 14 for codes)	S to N	Map
		Miles from *Delware Water Gap, PA*			*Miles from* *PA-MD line*	
		69.7	Pulpit Rock (1,582')		160.3	
		71.3	Windsor Furnace Shelter (940')	Sw	158.7	
		71.5	Windsor Furnace		158.5	
		74.1	Pocahontas Spring (1,200')			
			(w on A.T.; L,M 1m E)	LMw	155.9	
		76.7	Pa. 61			
			(M 0.5m W)	RM	153.3	
		77.4	**Port Clinton, Pa., P.O. 19549** (400')			
			(P.O. on A.T.; L,S 0.5m W; G,M,L 3m E)	RGLMS	152.6	
		81.4	Phillip's Canyon Spring (1,500')	w	148.6	
		84.1	Shartlesville Cross-Mountain Road;			
			Shartlesville, Pa., P.O. 19554			
			(P.O.,G,L,M 3.6m E)	RGLM	145.9	
		86.0	Eagle's Nest Shelter			
			(S,w 0.3m W)	Sw	144.0	
		86.7	Sand Spring Trail			
			(w 0.2m E)	w	143.3	
		90.5	Black Swatara Spring			
			(w 0.3m E)	w	139.5	
		91.8	Pa. 183, Rentschler Marker (1,440')	R	138.2	
		92.1	Fort Dietrich Snyder Marker			
			(w 0.2m W)	w	137.9	
		95.2	Shuberts Gap		134.8	
		95.3	Hertlein Campsite	Cw	134.7	
		97.8	Round Head and Shower Steps	w	132.2	
		100.4	Trail to Pilger Ruh Spring	Cw	129.6	
		100.9	Pa. 501; **Pine Grove, Pa., P.O. 17963,** 501 Shelter			
			(P.O.,M 3.7m W; S,w 0.1m W; G 4.3m W; L 5.7m W)	RGLMSw	129.1	

Left margin (vertical): Blue Mountain Eagle Climbing Club (BMECC) — Pa. Section 4, Pa. Section 5, Pa. Section 6

Right margin (vertical): KTA Sections 1–6 Map

Pennsylvania

Club	GBS	N to S	Features	Facilities (see page 14 for codes)	S to N	Map

Miles from
Delware Water Gap, PA

Miles from
PA-MD line

Club	GBS	N to S	Features	Facilities	S to N	Map
		102.8	Pa. 645	R	127.2	
	Pa. Section 6	105.0	Blue Mountain Spring,			KTA Sec. 1–6 Map
BMECC			William Penn Shelter (1,380')	Sw	125.0	
		111.9	I-81	R	118.1	
		112.3	Swatara Gap, Pa. 72 (480')			
			(C,G,L,M 2m E)	RGL	117.7	
	Pa. Section 7	113.7	Pa. 443; Green Point, Pa.	R	116.3	
		118.4	Rausch Gap Shelter (980') (S,w 0.3m E)	Sw	111.6	
		120.7	Cold Spring Trail		109.3	
Susquehanna A.T. Club		123.0	Yellow Springs Village Site		107.0	
		123.5	Yellow Springs Trail		106.5	
		126.4	Stony Mountain; Horse-Shoe Trail (1,650')		103.6	
		129.7	Pa. 325, Clarks Valley (550')	Rw	100.3	
		130.0	Spring	w	100.0	
	Pa. Section 8	132.3	Shikellimy Trail		97.7	KTA Sections 7–8 Map
		133.7	Kinter View (1,320')		96.3	
		134.8	Whitetail Trail		95.2	
		135.4	Victoria Trail		94.6	
		136.4	Peters Mountain Shelter	Sw	93.6	
		137.2	Table Rock		92.8	
		139.2	Pa. 225	R	90.8	
York HC		143.1	Clarks Ferry Shelter (1,260')	Sw	86.9	
		143.3	Campsite	Cw	86.7	
		145.5	U.S. 22 & 322, Norfolk Southern Railway	R	84.5	
		146.1	Clarks Ferry Bridge (west end),			
Mtn. Club of Maryland	Pa. Section 9		Susquehanna River (380')			PATC Map 1
			(C on A.T.; M 0.1m W)	RCM	83.9	
		146.3	Juniata River, Pa. 849	R	83.7	
		147.3	**Duncannon, Pa., P.O. 17020**			
			(P.O.,L,M on A.T., G 0.6m W)	RGLM	82.7	

Pennsylvania

Club	GBS	N to S	Features	Facilities (see page 14 for codes)	S to N	Map
			Miles from *Delware Water Gap, PA*		*Miles from* *PA-MD line*	
		147.8	U.S. 11 & 15, Pa. 274	R	82.2	
		149.5	Hawk Rock		80.5	
MCM	Pa. Section 9	151.4	Cove Mountain Shelter (1,200')	Sw	78.6	
		156.4	Pa. 850 (650')	R	73.6	
		158.7	Darlington Shelter (1,250')	Sw	71.3	
		158.8	Darlington Trail, Tuscarora Trail		71.2	
		159.7	Spring	w	70.3	
		160.7	Pa. 944 (480'); Donnellytown, Pa.	R	69.3	
		161.6	Sherwood Drive	Rw	68.4	
		162.7	Conodoguinet Creek, Scott Farm Trail Work Center	R	67.3	
Cumberland Valley A.T. Club	Pa. Section 10	164.1	I-81 Crossing	R	65.9	PATC Map 1
		165.0	U.S. 11; **Carlisle, Pa., P.O. 17013** **New Kingston, Pa., P.O. 17072** (P.O. 5m W; 1.7m E; G 1.3m E; L,M 0.3m W; M 0.3m E)	RGLM	65.0	
		166.2	Pennsylvania Turnpike	R	63.8	
		168.9	Trindle Road (Pa. 641)	R	61.1	
		171.0	Pa. 74	R	59.0	
		173.0	Pa. 174, **Boiling Springs, Pa., P.O. 17007** (P.O.,w on A.T.; G,L,M 0.1m W; G 1m W)	★ RGLMw	57.0	
	Pa. Section 11	173.3	Yellow Breeches Creek (500')	R	56.7	
		173.5	Backpackers' Campsite	Cw	56.5	
		176.0	Center Point Knob (1,060')		54.0	
		176.9	Alec Kennedy Shelter	Sw	53.1	
Mtn. Club of Md.	Pa. 12	179.0	Whiskey Spring, Whiskey Spring Road	Rw	51.0	
		181.8	Pa. 94 (880'); **Mount Holly Springs, Pa., P.O. 17065** (P.O.,G,M 2.5m W)	RGM	48.2	

Pennsylvania

Club	GBS	N to S	Features	Facilities (see page 14 for codes)	S to N	Map
		Miles from Delware Water Gap, PA			*Miles from PA-MD line*	
		183.6	Hunters Run Road (Pa. 34); **Gardners, Pa., P.O. 17324** (P.O. 5m E; G 0.2m E)	RG	46.4	
		184.5	Pine Grove Road (C,M 0.4m W)	RCM	45.5	
		185.0	James Fry (Tagg Run) Shelter (S,w 0.2m E)	Sw	45.0	
		186.2	Side trail to Mountain Creek Campground (C,G 0.7m W)	CG	43.8	
		186.4	Limekiln Road	R	43.6	
		189.7	Side trail to Pole Steeple (1,300')		40.3	
		192.2	Pine Grove Furnace State Park	RCGLw	37.8	
		192.5	Pa. 233 (900'), Appalachian Trail Museum	R	37.5	
		195.9	Toms Run Shelter	Sw	34.1	
		197.0	Woodrow Road	R	33.0	
		198.9	Michener Cabin (locked) (w 0.3m E)	w	31.1	
		200.8	Shippensburg Road (2,040')	R	29.2	
		202.1	Birch Run Shelter	Sw	27.9	
		204.5	Milesburn Road, Milesburn Cabin (locked)	Rw	25.5	
		204.9	Ridge Road, Means Hollow Road	R	25.1	
		205.4	Middle Ridge Road	R	24.6	
		208.0	Sandy Sod Junction (1,980')	R	22.0	
		209.5	Quarry Gap Shelters	Sw	20.5	
		210.2	Quarry Gap Road	R	19.8	
		212.1	U.S. 30, Caledonia State Park, Thaddeus Stevens Museum (960'); **Fayetteville, Pa., P.O. 17222** (P.O 3.9m W; C,w on A.T.; G 2.3m W; M 0.4m W; L 0.8mW)	RCGLMw	17.9	

Club column (left margin): Mountain Club of Maryland — Pa. Section 12; Potomac A.T. Club — Pa. Section 13, Pa. Section 14

Map column (right margin): PATC Maps 2-3

Pennsylvania

Club	GBS	N to S	Features	Facilities (see page 14 for codes)	S to N	Map
		Miles from Delware Water Gap, PA			*Miles from PA-MD line*	
		215.1	Rocky Mountain Shelters (S 0.2m E; w 0.5m E)	Sw	14.9	
		216.8	Pa. 233 (1,600'); **South Mountain, Pa., P.O. 17261** (P.O.,C,G,M 1.3m E)	RCGM	13.2	
		217.1	Swamp Road	R	12.9	
		220.4	Chimney Rocks (1,900')		9.6	
		221.7	Tumbling Run Shelters, Hermitage Cabin (locked)	Sw	8.3	
Potomac A.T. Club	Pa. Section 14	221.9	Old Forge Road (1,000')	R	8.1	PATC Map 4
		222.5	Rattlesnake Run Road	R	7.5	
		222.9	Old Forge Park	RCw	7.1	
		225.3	Deer Lick Shelters (1,420')	Sw	4.7	
		226.6	Bailey Spring	w	3.4	
		227.2	Mackie Run, Mentzer Gap Road	R	2.8	
		227.4	Pa. 16; **Blue Ridge Summit, Pa., P.O. 17214; Rouzerville, Pa., P.O. 17250; Waynesboro, Pa. P.O. 17268** (P.O.,G,M 1.3m E; P.O.,G,L,M 2.2m W, 5.7m W)	RGM	2.6	
		227.7	Old Pa. 16	R	2.3	
		228.9	Buena Vista Road	Rw	1.1	
		229.9	Pen Mar Road	R	0.1	
		230.0	Pennsylvania–Maryland Line (1,250')	R	0.0	

Club GBS	N to S	Features	Facilities (see page 14 for codes)	S to N	Map
	Miles from PA-MD line			*Miles from Front Royal, VA*	

	0.0	Pennsylvania–Maryland Line (1,250')	R	95.2	
	0.2	Pen Mar Park;			
		Cascade, Md., P.O. 21719			
		(P.O.,G,M 1.6m E; w on A.T.;			
		M 1.4m E)	RGMw	95.0	
	3.1	Trail to High Rock	R	92.1	
	4.9	Raven Rocks Shelter	CSw	90.3	
		(C,S 0.2m W; w 0.1m E)			
	5.9	Raven Rock Hollow, Md. 491	R	89.3	
	6.7	Warner Gap Road	Rw	88.5	
	8.5	Foxville Road (Md. 77)	R	86.7	
	9.8	Ensign Cowall Shelter	Sw	85.4	
	10.0	Wolfsville Road (Md. 17) (1,400');			
		Smithsburg, Md., P.O. 21783			
		(P.O.,G,M 2.4m W; L 6.4m W)	RGLM	85.2	
	14.8	Pogo Memorial Campsite	Cw	80.4	
	15.4	Black Rock Cliffs (1,800')		79.8	
	16.4	Trail to Annapolis Rock			
		(C 0.2m W; w 0.4m W)	Cw	78.8	
	18.0	Pine Knob Shelter	CSw	77.2	
	18.6	I-70 Footbridge, U.S. 40			
		(C 1.4m W; M,w 0.5m W)	RCMw	76.6	
	19.4	Boonsboro Mountain Road	R	75.8	
	21.5	Washington Monument		73.7	
	21.9	Washington Monument Road	Rw	73.3	
	22.1	Monument Road	R	73.1	
	23.5	Turners Gap, U.S. Alt. 40 (1,000');			
		Boonsboro, Md., P.O. 21713	★		
		(M on A.T; P.O.,M 2.3m W;			
		G 1.6m W, 3.7m W)	RGM	71.7	

Md. Section 1 · Md. Section 2 · Md. Section 3 · Md. Section 4 · Md. Sec. 5

Potomac A.T. Club

PATC Maps 5-6

Maryland–West Virginia–Northern Virginia

Club	GBS	N to S	Features	Facilities (see page 14 for codes)	S to N	Map
		Miles from PA-MD line			*Miles from Front Royal, VA*	
		23.7	Dahlgren Back Pack Campground	Cw	71.5	
		24.5	Reno Monument Road	R	70.7	
		25.5	Rocky Run Shelter (C,S,w 0.2m W)	CSw	69.7	
	Md. Section 5	27.1	Lambs Knoll (1,600')		68.1	
		27.3	White Rocks Cliff		67.9	
		27.9	Trail to Bear Spring Cabin (locked) (w 0.5m E)	w	67.3	
		30.5	Crampton Gap Shelter (C,S,w 0.3m E)	CSw	64.7	
Potomac A.T. Club	Md. Section 6	30.9	Crampton Gap, Gathland State Park, Gapland Road (Md. 572) (950'); **Burkittsville, Md., P.O. 21718** (P.O. 1.2m E; w on A.T.)	Rw	64.3	PATC Maps 5-6
		32.6	Brownsville Gap		62.6	
		34.6	Ed Garvey Shelter (S on A.T.; w 0.4m E)	Sw	60.6	
		36.7	Trail to Weverton Cliffs		58.5	
		37.6	Weverton Road (G 1.4m W)	RG	57.6	
	Md. Section 7	37.8	U.S. 340 Underpass		57.4	
		38.0	Keep Tryst Road (L,M 1.2m W)	RLM	57.2	
		38.1	C&O Canal Towpath (east junction)		57.1	
		39.6	U.S. 340, Sandy Hook Bridge		55.6	
	Sec. 8	40.7	C&O Canal Towpath (west junction)		54.5	
		40.9	Potomac River, Goodloe Byron Memorial Footbridge, Maryland–West Virginia Line (250')		54.3	

Maryland–West Virginia–Northern Virginia

Club	GBS	N to S	Features	Facilities (see page 14 for codes)	S to N	Map
		Miles from PA-MD line			*Miles from Front Royal, VA*	
		41.0	Shenandoah Street; Harpers Ferry National Historical Park (M 0.1m W)	RM	54.2	
		41.6	Appalachian Trail Conservancy Side Trail; **Harpers Ferry, W.Va., P.O. 25425** (P.O. 0.5m W; G 1.1m W; L 0.6m W; M 0.4m W; ATC 0.2m W)	★ RGLM	53.6	
		41.9	U.S. 340, Shenandoah River Bridge (north end) (L 0.1m W; C 1.2m W)	RCL	53.3	
		42.6	Chestnut Hill Road (W.Va. 32)	R	52.6	
		43.1	Loudoun Heights Trail to Split Rock		52.1	
		43.3	West Virginia–Virginia Line (1,200')		51.9	
		45.6	Four Mile Campsite	C(nw)	49.6	
		47.5	Keys Gap, W.Va. 9 (G,M,w 0.3m W, 0.3m E)	RGMw	47.7	
		50.5	David Lesser Memorial Shelter (S 0.1m E; C,w 0.3m E)	CSw	44.7	
		53.7	Trail to Blackburn Trail Center (1,650') (C 0.1m E; S,w 0.3m E)	CSw	41.5	
		54.9	Wilson Gap		40.3	
		57.8	Devils Racecourse		37.4	
		57.9	Sand Spring	w	37.3	
		58.5	Crescent Rock		36.7	
		58.6	West Virginia–Virginia Line		36.6	
		58.9	Spring	w	36.3	
		61.1	Snickers Gap, Va. 7, Va. 679 (1,000'); **Bluemont, Va., P.O. 20135** (P.O. 1.7m E; G 1m W; M 0.3m W, 0.9m W)	★ RGM	34.1	

Club: Potomac A.T. Club

GBS: W.Va.–Va. Section 1 · W.Va.–Va. Section 2 · W.Va.–Va. Section 3 · Va. Sec. 3

Map: PATC Map 7

Maryland–West Virginia–Northern Virginia

Club	GBS	N to S	Features	Facilities (see page 14 for codes)	S to N	Map
		Miles from PA-MD line		*Miles from Front Royal, VA*		
		61.7	Bears Den Rocks, Bears Den Hostel (L,w 0.2m E)	Lw	33.5	
		64.7	Sawmill Spring, Sam Moore Shelter	Sw	30.5	
	Va. Section 3	66.7	Spring	w	28.5	
		67.9	Morgans Mill Road (Va. 605)	R	27.3	
		71.1	Fisher Loop Trail (north junction)		24.1	
		71.6	Rod Hollow Shelter	Sw	23.6	
		71.9	Fisher Loop Trail (south junction)		23.3	
		75.2	Ashby Gap, U.S. 50 (900') (G,M 0.8m W; L 4m W; L,M 1.2m E)	RLM	20.0	
Potomac A.T. Club	Va. Section 4	77.8	Sky Meadows State Park Side Trail (C,w 1.3m E)	Cw	17.4	PATC Map 8
		79.0	Spring	w	16.2	
		80.0	Whiskey Hollow Shelter (S,w 0.2m E)	Sw	15.2	
		82.6	Trillium Trail (1,900')		12.6	
		84.5	Manassas Gap Shelter	Sw	10.7	
		87.0	Va. 55 (800'); **Linden, Va., P.O. 22642** (P.O.,G 1m W)	RG	8.2	
	Va. Section 5	88.9	Va. 638	R	6.3	
		90.0	Jim & Molly Denton Shelter	CSw	5.2	
		91.9	Mosby Campsite, Tom Sealock Spring (1,800')	Cw	3.3	
		95.2	U.S. 522 (950'); **Front Royal, Va., P.O. 22630** (P.O.,G 4.2m W; G,M 3.2m W; L,M 3.6m W)	★ RGLM	0.0	

Club	GBS	N to S	Features	Facilities (see page 14 for codes)	S to N	Map
		Miles from Front Royal, VA			*Miles from Rockfish Gap, VA*	
		0.0	U.S. 522 (950');			
			Front Royal, Va., P.O. 22630	★		
			(P.O.,G 4.2m W; G,M 3.2m W;			
			L,M 3.6m W)	RGLM	107.8	
		1.4	Va. 602	R	106.4	
		2.9	Tom Floyd Wayside	Sw	104.9	
		3.6	Possums Rest Overlook,			
			SNP northern boundary; self-registration			
			station for SNP camping permits		104.2	
		3.8	Compton Gap Horse Trail		104.0	
		5.3	Indian Run Spring			
			(w 0.3m E)	w	102.5	
		5.6	Compton Gap; Skyline Drive, mile 10.4	R	102.2	
		6.4	Compton Peak (2,909')		101.4	
		6.8	Compton Springs	w	101.0	
		7.7	Jenkins Gap; Skyline Drive, mile 12.3	R	100.1	
		9.4	Hogwallow Gap;			
			Skyline Drive, mile 14.2 (2,739')	R	98.4	
		10.0	Hogwallow Spring	w	97.8	
		10.9	North Marshall Mountain (3,368')		96.9	
		11.6	Skyline Drive, mile 15.9	R	96.2	
		12.1	South Marshall Mountain (3,212')		95.7	
		13.2	Gravel Springs Gap;			
			Skyline Drive, mile 17.7 (2,666')	R	94.6	
		13.4	Gravel Springs Hut			
			(S,w 0.2m E)	Sw	94.4	
		14.5	Skyline Drive, mile 18.9	R	93.3	
		15.0	Little Hogback Mountain		92.8	
		15.1	Little Hogback Overlook;			
			Skyline Drive, mile 19.7	R	92.7	

Potomac A.T. Club

SNP Section 1 (Va. 6)

SNP Section 2 (Va. 7)

PATC Map 9

Shenandoah National Park

Club	GBS	N to S	Features	Facilities (see page 14 for codes)	S to N	Map
		Miles from Front Royal, VA			*Miles from Rockfish Gap, VA*	
		15.8	First peak of Hogback		92.0	
		15.9	Spring			
			(w 0.2m E)	w	91.9	
		16.1	Second peak of Hogback (3,475')		91.7	
		16.3	Skyline Drive, mile 20.8	R	91.5	
		16.4	Third peak of Hogback		91.4	
		16.6	Skyline Drive, mile 21.1	R	91.2	
		17.0	Tuscarora Trail		90.8	
		17.6	Rattlesnake Point Overlook;			
			Skyline Drive, mile 21.9	R	90.2	
		18.3	Range View Cabin (locked)	w	89.5	
			(w 0.1m E)			
		19.1	Elkwallow Gap;			
			Skyline Drive, mile 23.9 (2,480')			
			(G,M 0.1m E)	RGM	88.7	
		19.6	Spring	w	88.2	
		24.2	Byrds Nest #4 Picnic Shelter			
			(0.5m E)	w	83.6	
		24.3	Beahms Gap; Skyline Drive, mile 28.5	R	83.5	
		24.6	Skyline Drive, mile 28.6	R	83.2	
		25.7	Pass Mountain (3,052')		82.1	
		26.5	Pass Mountain Hut			
			(S,w 0.2m E)	Sw	81.3	
		27.7	Thornton Gap, U.S. 211;			
			Skyline Drive, mile 31.5 (2,307')	R	80.1	
		29.6	Marys Rock (3,514')		78.2	
		30.2	Meadow Spring			
			(w 0.3m E)	w	77.6	
		30.9	Byrds Nest #3 Shelter (w 0.3m E)	S	76.9	
		31.9	The Pinnacle (3,730')		75.9	

Club: Potomac A.T. Club

GBS: SNP Section 2 (Va. 7) / SNP Section 3 (Va. 8)

Map: PATC Map 9 / PATC Map 10

Shenandoah National Park

Club	GBS	N to S	Features	Facilities (see page 14 for codes)	S to N	Map
			Miles from Front Royal, VA	*Miles from Rockfish Gap, VA*		
		32.9	Side trail to Jewell Hollow Overlook; Skyline Drive, mile 36.4	R	74.9	
		33.0	Pinnacles Picnic Ground; Skyline Drive, mile 36.7	Rw	74.8	
		35.2	Hughes River Gap; side trail to Stony Man Mountain Overlook; Skyline Drive, mile 38.6 (3,097')	Rw	72.6	
		36.8	Side trail to Stony Man summit		71.0	
		37.2	Skyland Service Road (north) (L,M 0.3m W)	RLM	70.6	
		38.0	Skyland Service Road (south)	R	69.8	
		40.1	Side trail to Crescent Rock Overlook; Skyline Drive, mile 44.4	R	67.7	
		40.5	Hawksbill Gap; Skyline Drive, mile 45.6 (3,361')	R	67.3	
		41.5	Side trail to Hawksbill Mountain, Byrd's Nest #2 Picnic Shelter (0.9m E)		66.3	
		41.8	Rock Spring Cabin (locked) & Hut (S,w 0.2m W)	Sw	66.0	
		43.7	Fishers Gap; Skyline Drive, mile 49.3	R	64.1	
		44.7	David Spring	w	63.1	
		45.3	Big Meadows (3,500') (C,L,M 0.1m E)	RCLM	62.5	
		46.2	Big Meadows Wayside, Harry F. Byrd, Sr., Visitor Center (w on A.T.; G,M 0.4m E)	RGMw	61.6	
		47.0	Spring	w	60.8	
		47.9	Milam Gap; Skyline Drive, mile 52.8	R	59.9	
		49.8	Hazeltop (3,812')		58.0	

Left margin labels: Potomac A.T. Club — SNP Section 3 (Va. 8), SNP Section 4 (Va. 9), SNP Section 5 (Va. 10)

Right margin label: PATC Map 10

Shenandoah National Park

Club	GBS	N to S	Features	Facilities (see page 14 for codes)	S to N	Map
			Miles from Front Royal, VA		*Miles from Rockfish Gap, VA*	
		50.7	Bootens Gap; Skyline Drive, mile 55.1 (3,243')	R	57.1	
		53.3	Bearfence Mountain Hut (S,w 0.1m E)	Sw	54.5	
	SNP Section 5 (Va. 10)	54.0	Lewis Mountain Campground; Skyline Drive, mile 57.6 (C,G,L,w 0.1m W)	RCGLw	53.8	PATC Map 10
		55.7	Spring	w	52.1	
		56.0	Pocosin Cabin (locked)	w	51.8	
		59.3	South River Picnic Grounds (w 0.1m W)	w	48.5	
Potomac A.T. Club		62.3	Swift Run Gap, U.S. 33; Skyline Drive, mile 65.5 (2,367')	R	45.5	
		63.6	Skyline Drive, mile 66.7	R	44.2	
		65.1	Hightop Mountain (3,587')		42.7	
	SNP Section 6 (Va. 11)	65.2	Spring	w	42.6	
		65.7	Hightop Hut (S 0.1m W; w 0.2m W)	Sw	42.1	
		66.9	Smith Roach Gap; Skyline Drive, mile 68.6	R	40.9	PATC Map 11
		68.1	Little Roundtop Mountain		39.7	
		68.5	Powell Gap; Skyline Drive, mile 69.9 (2,294')	R	39.3	
		71.8	Simmons Gap; Skyline Drive, mile 73.2	Rw	36.0	
	SNP Sec. 7 (Va. 12)	73.7	Pinefield Gap; Skyline Drive, mile 75.2	R	34.1	
		73.9	Pinefield Hut	Sw	33.9	
		75.5	Ivy Creek Overlook; Skyline Drive, mile 77.5	R	32.3	
		77.6	Spring (w 0.1m W)	w	30.2	

Shenandoah National Park

Club	GBS	N to S	Features	Facilities (see page 14 for codes)	S to N	Map
			Miles from Front Royal, VA	*Miles from Rockfish Gap, VA*		
		79.7	Loft Mountain Campground (3,300') (C,G,M,w 0.2m W)	CGMw	28.1	
		81.8	Doyles River Cabin (locked); Skyline Drive, mile 81.1 (w 0.3m E)	Rw	26.0	
		82.7	Doyles River Parking Overlook; Skyline Drive, mile 81.9	R	25.1	
		83.1	Skyline Drive, mile 82.2	R	24.7	
		84.0	Browns Gap; Skyline Drive, mile 82.9 (2,600')	R	23.8	
		85.5	Skyline Drive, mile 84.3	R	22.3	
		86.5	Blackrock (3,100')		21.3	
		87.1	Blackrock Hut (S,w 0.2m E)	Sw	20.7	
		87.6	Skyline Drive, mile 87.2	R	20.2	
		87.8	Blackrock Gap; Skyline Drive, mile 87.4 (2,321')	R	20.0	
		89.6	Skyline Drive, mile 88.9	R	18.2	
		93.7	Skyline Drive, mile 92.4 (3,100')	R	14.1	
		95.7	Turk Gap; Skyline Drive, mile 94.1	R	12.1	
		97.3	Skyline Drive, mile 95.3	R	10.5	
		98.9	Spring	w	8.9	
		99.1	Jarman Gap; Skyline Drive, mile 96.9; SNP southern boundary (2,173')	R	8.7	
		99.5	Spring	w	8.3	
		100.1	Calf Mountain Shelter (w 0.2m W; S 0.3m W)	Sw	7.7	
		102.3	Beagle Gap; Skyline Drive, mile 99.5	R	5.5	
		102.8	Bear Den Mountain (2,885')		5.0	
		104.1	McCormick Gap; Skyline Drive, mile 102.1	R	3.7	

Column labels (vertical):
- Potomac A.T. Club
- SNP Section 7 (Va. 12)
- SNP Section 8 (Va. 13)
- SNP Sec. 9 (Va. 14)
- PATC Map 11

Shenandoah National Park

Club	GBS	N to S	Features	Facilities (see page 14 for codes)	S to N	Map
			Miles from *Front Royal, VA*	*Miles from* *Rockfish Gap, VA*		
Potomac A.T. Club	SNP Sec. 9 (Va. 14)	107.0	Self-registration for SNP camping permits, park entrance station			PATC Map 11
			(0.2m W)		0.8	
		107.5	Skyline Drive, mile 105.2	R	0.3	
		107.7	I-64 Overpass		0.1	
		107.8	Rockfish Gap, U.S. 250, I-64 (1,902');			
			Waynesboro, Va., P.O. 22980	★		
			(P.O.,G,L,M 4.5m W; G,L,M on A.T.)	RGLM	0.0	

Club	GBS	N to S	Features	Facilities (see page 14 for codes)	S to N	Map
			Miles from Rockfish Gap, VA		*Miles from New River, VA*	
		0.0	Rockfish Gap, U.S. 250, I-64 (1,902'); **Waynesboro, Va., P.O. 22980** (P.O.,G,L,M 4.5m W)	★ RGLM	226.8	
		4.8	Mill Creek, Paul C. Wolfe Shelter	Sw	222.0	
		6.1	Jack Albright Trail		220.7	
		6.5	Side trail to Glass Hollow Overlook		220.3	
		7.4	Side trail to Humpback Rocks Visitors Center (w 0.5m W)	w	219.4	
Old Dominion A.T. Club	Va. Section 15	9.7	Bear Spring	w	217.1	
		10.3	Side trail to Humpback Rocks		216.5	
		11.5	Humpback Mountain (3,606')		215.3	
		14.3	Dripping Rock Parking Area; Blue Ridge Parkway, mile 9.6	Rw	212.5	Central Va. Map 1
		14.8	Cedar Cliffs		212.0	
		18.6	Three Ridges Overlook; Blue Ridge Parkway, mile 13.1	R	208.2	
		19.1	Reids Gap (2,645'), Va. 664; Blue Ridge Parkway, mile 13.6	R	207.7	
		20.8	Maupin Field Shelter	Sw	206.0	
Tidewater A.T. Club	Va. Section 16	22.8	Hanging Rock Overlook		204.0	
		23.3	Three Ridges Mountain (3,970')		203.5	
		25.0	Chimney Rocks		201.8	
		27.0	Harpers Creek Shelter	Sw	199.8	
		29.7	Tye River	Cw	197.1	
		29.8	Va. 56 (997') (C,L 4.1m W)	RCL	197.0	
NBATC	Va. Section 17	31.1	Cripple Creek	w	195.7	
		34.1	The Priest (4,063')		192.7	
		34.6	The Priest Shelter	Sw	192.2	

Central Virginia

Club	GBS	N to S	Features	Facilities	S to N	Map
			Miles from Rockfish Gap, VA		*Miles from New River, VA*	
		35.5	Meadows Lane (Va. 826), Crabtree Falls Trail (C,w 0.5m W; C,L 4.1m E)	RCLw	191.3	
	Va. Section 17	36.3	Cash Hollow Road (3,280'); **Montebello, Va., P.O. 24464** (P.O.,C,G,L 4.5m W)	RCGL	190.5	
		37.6	Cash Hollow Rock		189.2	
		38.4	Spy Rock		188.4	
		38.9	Spy Rock Road (3,454')		187.9	
		40.1	Porters Field	Cw	186.7	
	Va. Section 18	41.2	Seeley-Woodworth Shelter	Sw	185.6	
		41.9	Elk Pond Branch	Cw	184.9	Central Va. Map 1
Natural Bridge A.T. Club (NBATC)		43.1	North Fork of Piney River	Cw	183.7	
		45.0	Greasy Spring Road	R	181.8	
		45.5	USFS 246	R	181.3	
		46.7	Salt Log Gap (north), USFS 63 (3,290')	R	180.1	
	Va. Section 19	48.0	Tar Jacket Ridge (3,840')		178.8	
		48.9	Hog Camp Gap, USFS 48 (3,485')	RCw	177.9	
		50.2	Cole Mountain (4,022')		176.6	
		51.4	Old Hotel Trail, Cow Camp Gap Shelter (3,428') (S,w 0.6m E)	Sw	175.4	
		52.4	Bald Knob (4,059')		174.4	
	Va. Section 20	55.2	Long Mountain Wayside, U.S. 60 (2,060'); **Buena Vista, Va., P.O. 24416** (P.O.,C,G,L,M 9.3m W)	★ RCGLM	171.6	
		57.0	Brown Mountain Creek Shelter	Sw	169.8	
		59.0	Swapping Camp Road (USFS 38)	R	167.8	C. Va. Map 2
		61.9	Pedlar River Bridge	w	164.9	
		62.0	USFS 39	R	164.8	

Central Virginia

Club	GBS	N to S	Features	Facilities (see page 14 for codes)	S to N	Map
			Miles from Rockfish Gap, VA	*Miles from New River, VA*		
		63.9	Rice Mountain (2,169')		162.9	
		65.8	Robinson Gap Road (Va. 607)	R	161.0	
		66.1	Blue Ridge Parkway, mile 51.7; Punchbowl Mountain Crossing (2,170')	Rw	160.7	
		66.5	Punchbowl Shelter (S,w 0.2m W)	Sw	160.3	
		67.0	Punchbowl Mountain		159.8	
		68.1	Bluff Mountain (3,391')		158.7	
		69.6	Saltlog Gap (south) (2,573')		157.2	
		70.7	Saddle Gap, Saddle Gap Trail		156.1	
		72.2	Big Rocky Row (2,974')		154.6	
		73.2	Fullers Rocks, Little Rocky Row (2,486')		153.6	
		73.3	Rocky Row Trail		153.5	
		75.3	Johns Hollow Shelter	Sw	151.5	
		75.9	Va. 812 (USFS 36)	R	150.9	
		76.0	Rocky Row Run (760')	Cw	150.8	
		76.9	Lower Rocky Row Run bridge	w	149.9	
		77.0	U.S. 501, Va. 130; **Big Island, Va., P.O. 24526; Glasgow, Va., P.O. 24555** (P.O.,G,M 5.6m E; P.O.,C,G,L,M,S 5.9m W; C,L 4.8m E)	★ RCGLMS	149.8	
		77.2	James River Foot Bridge (678')		149.6	
		78.4	Campsite	Cw	148.4	
		79.2	Matts Creek Shelter	Sw	147.6	
		81.1	Big Cove Branch	w	145.7	
		81.9	Sulphur Spring Trail (north crossing) (2,588')		144.9	
		82.4	Hickory Stand, Gunter Ridge Trail		144.4	

Left margin labels: *Natural Bridge A.T. Club*, *Va. Section 21*, *Va. Section 22*
Right margin label: *Central Va. Map 2*

Central Virginia

Club	GBS	N to S	Features	Facilities	S to N	Map
		Miles from Rockfish Gap, VA			*Miles from New River, VA*	
	Va. Sec. 22	84.2	Sulphur Spring Trail (south crossing)		142.6	
		84.7	Marble Spring	Cw	142.1	
		85.9	Highcock Knob (3,054')		140.9	
		87.1	Petites Gap, USFS 35; Blue Ridge Parkway, mile 71.0 (2,369')	R	139.7	
		88.5	Harrison Ground Spring	w	138.3	
	Va. Section 23	90.4	Thunder Ridge Overlook; Blue Ridge Parkway, mile 74.7 (3,525')	R	136.4	
		90.8	Lower Blue Ridge Parkway crossing, mile 74.9	R	136.0	
Natural Bridge A.T. Club		91.8	Thunder Hill Shelter	Sw	135.0	
		92.1	Upper Blue Ridge Parkway crossing, mile 76.3	R	134.7	Central Va. Map 2
		92.7	The Guillotine		134.1	
		93.0	Apple Orchard Mountain (4,206')		133.8	
	Va. Section 24	94.4	Parkers Gap Road (USFS 812); Blue Ridge Parkway, mile 78.4 (3,410')	R	132.4	
		94.5	Apple Orchard Falls Trail		132.3	
		96.2	Black Rock side trail		130.6	
		97.1	Cornelius Creek Shelter	Sw	129.7	
		97.7	Floyd Mountain (3,560')		129.1	
		102.0	Bryant Ridge Shelter (1,330')	Sw	124.8	
		104.2	Fork Mountain (2,042')		122.6	
	Va. Section 25	105.8	Va. 614, Jennings Creek (987') (w on A.T.; C,G,L,M 1.6m E, M 4.5m W)	RCGLMw	121.0	
		107.3	Buchanan Trail		119.5	
		109.0	Cove Mountain Shelter	S(nw)	117.8	
		110.4	Little Cove Mountain Trail		116.4	

Central Virginia

Club	GBS	N to S	Features	Facilities	S to N	Map
		Miles from Rockfish Gap, VA			*Miles from New River, VA*	
		110.8	Cove Mountain (2,707')		116.0	
		112.4	Bearwallow Gap, Va. 43, Blue Ridge Parkway, mile 90.9 (2,228'); **Buchanan, Va., P.O. 24066** (P.O.,G,M 5m W; M 7m W; C,L,M 4.9m E)	RCGLM	114.4	Central Va. Map 2
		114.1	Blue Ridge Parkway, mile 91.8; Mills Gap Overlook	R	112.7	
		114.8	Blue Ridge Parkway, mile 92.5; Peaks of Otter Overlook	R	112.0	
Natural Bridge A.T. Club	Va. Section 26	115.5	Bobblets Gap Shelter (S,w 0.2m W)	Sw	111.3	
		117.9	Blue Ridge Parkway, mile 95.3; Harveys Knob Overlook	R	108.9	
		118.5	Blue Ridge Parkway, mile 95.9; Montvale Overlook	R	108.3	
		119.6	Blue Ridge Parkway, mile 97.0; Taylors Mountain Overlook	R	107.2	
		120.4	Black Horse Gap, Old Fincastle Road (USFS 186); Blue Ridge Parkway, mile 97.7 (2,402')	R	106.4	Central Va. Map 3
		122.4	Spring	w	104.4	
		122.8	Wilson Creek Shelter	Sw	104.0	
Roanoke A.T. Club	Va. Section 27	123.5	Wilson Creek	w	103.3	
		125.4	Curry Creek	w	101.4	
		126.2	Salt Pond Road (USFS 191)	R	100.6	
		129.0	Fullhardt Knob Shelter (2,676')	Sw	97.8	
		132.0	Va. 652 (Mountain Pass Road)	R	94.8	
		132.5	Norfolk Southern Railway, U.S. 11; **Troutville, Va., P.O. 24175** (P.O. 0.8m W; G 1.2m W; L,M 1m E)	★ RGLM	94.3	

Central Virginia

		Miles from Rockfish Gap, VA			Miles from New River, VA	
		132.8	Va. 779, I-81		94.0	
			(L 0.1m W)	RL		
		134.0	U.S. 220;			
			Daleville, Va., P.O. 24083;			
			(P.O. 1m W; G,L,M on A.T.)	RGLM	92.8	
		134.5	Tinker Creek (1,165')		92.3	
		138.0	Hay Rock, Tinker Ridge		88.8	
		139.1	Angels Gap		87.7	
		143.1	Lamberts Meadow Campsite, Sawmill Run	Cw	83.7	
		143.4	Lamberts Meadow Shelter	Sw	83.4	
		144.0	Scorched Earth Gap, Andy Layne Trail		82.8	
		144.5	Tinker Cliffs (3,000')		82.3	
		146.3	Brickey's Gap		80.5	
Roanoke A.T. Club	Va. Section 28	149.4	Campbell Shelter	Sw	77.4	Central Va. Map 3
		149.5	Pig Farm Campsite	Cw	77.3	
		150.1	McAfee Knob (3,199')		76.7	
		151.4	Fire Road Connector Trail north junction		75.4	
		151.8	Catawba Mountain Shelter	Sw	75.0	
		152.8	Johns Spring Shelter	S	74.0	
		153.5	Fire Road Connector Trail south junction		73.3	
		153.8	Va. 311; **Catawba, Va., P.O. 24070**			
			(P.O. 1m W)	R	73.0	
		154.4	Catawba Greenway		72.4	
		158.1	Va. 785 (Blacksburg Road) (1,790')	R	68.7	
	Va. Section 29	159.7	Va. 624 (Newport Road), North Mountain Trail			
			(G 0.4m W; L 0.4m E)	RGL	67.1	
		160.7	Rawies Rest		66.1	
		161.2	Lost Spectacles Gap		65.6	
		162.2	Dragons Tooth, Cove Mountain (3,020')		64.6	

Central Virginia

Club	GBS	N to S	Features	Facilities (see page 14 for codes)	S to N	Map
			Miles from Rockfish Gap, VA	*Miles from New River, VA*		
	Va. Section 29	166.4	Pickle Branch Shelter (S,w 0.3m E)	Sw	60.4	Cent. Va. Map 3
		167.6	Trout Creek, Va. 620 (Miller Cove Road) (1,525')	R	59.2	
		171.4	Audie Murphy Monument (3,100')		55.4	
		175.2	Craig Creek Valley, Va. 621 (1,560')	R	51.6	
	Va. Section 30	176.5	Niday Shelter	Sw	50.3	
		178.9	Sinking Creek Mountain (3,490')		47.9	
Roanoke A.T. Club		182.5	Sarver Hollow Shelter (S,w 0.4m E)	Sw	44.3	
		185.8	Va. 630, Sinking Creek (2,100')	Rw	41.0	
		186.7	Sinking Creek Valley, Va. 42	R	40.1	
	Va. Section 31	189.1	Laurel Creek Shelter	Sw	37.7	
		192.1	Rocky Gap, Va. 601	R	34.7	
		193.1	Stream	w	33.7	
		194.1	Johns Creek Valley, USFS 156 (2,102')	Rw	32.7	Central Va. Map 4
		194.9	War Spur Shelter	Sw	31.9	
		198.6	Campsites, spring	Cw	28.2	
		199.8	Wind Rock (4,121')		27.0	
	Va. Section 32	200.0	Mountain Lake Road Salt Sulphur Turnpike (Va. 613)	R	26.8	
		203.7	Bailey Gap Shelter	S	23.1	
		203.9	Spring	w	22.9	
		205.2	Va. 635 (Big Stony Creek Road), Stony Creek (2,450')	R	21.6	
		206.2	Dismal Branch	w	20.6	
		207.3	Va. 635 (Big Stony Creek Road), Stony Creek Valley	R	19.5	
		207.6	Pine Swamp Branch Shelter	Sw	19.2	
		210.1	Allegheny Trail		16.7	

Central Virginia

Club	GBS	N to S	Features	Facilities (see page 14 for codes)	S to N	Map
		Miles from Rockfish Gap, VA			*Miles from New River, VA*	
		210.3	Peters Mountain (3,860')		16.5	
		212.5	Dickenson Gap		14.3	
		214.1	Groundhog Trail		12.7	
		215.1	Symms Gap Meadow		11.7	
		218.6	Campsite, spring	Cw	8.2	
		220.1	Rice Field Shelter (3,400')	S(nw)	6.7	
		220.7	Spring	w	6.1	
		221.7	Stream	w	5.1	
		222.9	Clendennin Road (Va. 641)	R	3.9	
		223.4	Hemlock Ridge		3.4	
		226.8	U.S. 460, Senator Shumate Bridge (east end), New River (1,600')	R	0.0	

Outdoor Club of Virginia Tech

Va. Section 33

Central Va. Map 4

Club	GBS	N to S	Features	Facilities (see page 14 for codes)	S to N	Map
		Miles from New River, VA			*Miles from Damascus, VA*	
		0.0	U.S. 460, Senator Shumate Bridge (east end), New River (1,600')	R	166.8	
		0.4	Va. 100, **Pearisburg, Va., P.O. 24134** (P.O.,G,L,M 1.3m E)	★ RGLM	166.4	
		1.4	Va. 634	R	165.4	
		3.4	Angels Rest, Pearis Mountain (3,550')		163.4	
		3.9	Campsite, spring	Cw	162.9	
		9.8	Doc's Knob Shelter	Sw	157.0	
Roanoke A.T. Club	Va. Section 34	12.1	Sugar Run Gap, Sugar Run Gap Rd. (Va. 663) (L 0.5m E)	RL	154.7	SW Va. Map 1
		13.7	Big Horse Gap, USFS 103 (3,752')	R	153.1	
		13.8	Ribble Trail, north junction	w	153.0	
		19.3	Wapiti Shelter (2,600')	Sw	147.5	
		21.1	Stream	w	145.7	
		21.4	Ribble Trail, south junction		145.4	
		23.5	Walnut Flats Campground (C,w 0.4m W)	Cw	143.3	
		25.4	Dismal Creek Falls Trail		141.4	
	Va. Sec. 35	27.3	Va. 606 (2,040') (C,G,M,w 0.5m W; L,M 0.5m E)	RCGLMw	139.5	
		27.4	Kimberling Creek		139.4	
		29.2	Brushy Mountain (2,800')		137.6	
	Va. Section 36	32.6	Va. 608, Lickskillet Hollow (2,200')	R	134.2	
		33.8	Jenny Knob Shelter	Sw	133.0	
		35.5	Brushy Mountain (3,101')		131.3	
		36.9	Va. 611	R	129.9	
OCVT		43.5	Helveys Mill Shelter (S,w 0.3m E)	Sw	123.3	Map 2
		44.9	Va. 612, Kimberling Creek	R	121.9	

Southwest Virginia

Club	GBS	N to S	Features	Facilities (see page 14 for codes)	S to N	Map
		Miles from New River, VA			*Miles from Damascus, VA*	
		45.3	I-77 Crossing	R	121.5	
		45.7	U.S. 52 (2,920'); **Bastian, Va., P.O. 24314; Bland, Va., P.O. 24315**	★		
			(P.O. 1.8m W; P.O.,G,L,M 2.7m E)	RGLM	121.1	
	Va. Section 37	50.5	Trail Boss Trail		116.3	
		52.6	Va. 615, Laurel Creek (2,450')	RCw	114.2	
		53.4	Brushy Mountain (3,080')		113.4	
		57.0	Jenkins Shelter (2,470')	Sw	109.8	
		57.9	Stream	w	108.9	
Piedmont A.T. Hikers		60.5	Davis Farm Campsite (C,w 0.4m W)	Cw	106.3	SW Va. Map 2
		61.5	Va. 623, Garden Mountain (3,880')	R	105.3	
		66.3	Walker Gap (3,520') (w 0.2m E)	Rw	100.5	
	Va. Section 38	67.7	Chestnut Knob Shelter (4,409')	S(nw)	99.1	
		69.5	Spring-fed pond	w	97.3	
		72.3	USFS 222 (2,300')	R	94.5	
		73.7	Lick Creek (ford)	w	93.1	
		76.0	Lynn Camp Creek (2,400')	w	90.8	
		76.6	Campsite, stream	Cw	90.2	
		77.1	Knot Maul Branch Shelter	S	89.7	
		78.3	Brushy Mountain (3,200')		88.5	
		79.2	Va. 42; **Ceres, Va., P.O. 24318**	R	87.6	
		79.8	Spring	w	87.0	
	Va. Section 39	80.2	Va. 742, North Fork of Holston River		86.6	
		81.7	Va. 610	R	85.1	
		83.2	Tilson Gap, Big Walker Mountain (3,500')		83.6	Map 3
		85.1	Crawfish Valley (2,600')	Cw	81.7	
		86.2	Little Brushy Mountain (3,300')		80.6	

Southwest Virginia

Club	GBS	NtoS	Features	Facilities (see page 14 for codes)	StoN	Map
			Miles from New River, VA		*Miles from Damascus, VA*	
		89.0	Davis Path Campsite	C(nw)	77.8	
		90.1	Spring	w	76.7	
		90.8	Va. 617	R	76.0	
		91.8	Va. 683, U.S. 11, I-81 (2,420');			
			Atkins, Va., P.O. 24311			
			(P.O. 3.1m W; G,L,M on A.T.)	RGLM	75.0	
		94.1	Va. 729	R	72.7	
		94.6	Va. 615	R	72.2	
		96.1	USFS 644	R	70.7	
		96.4	Chatfield Shelter	Sw	70.4	
		97.9	Glade Mountain (4,093')		68.9	
		99.2	USFS 86	Cw	67.6	
		99.6	Locust Mountain		67.2	
		100.6	Brushy Mountain		66.2	
		102.5	Va. 622	R	64.3	
		103.2	Va. 16 (3,220');			
			Sugar Grove, Va., P.O. 24375			
			Marion, Va., P.O. 24354	★		
			(P.O.,G 3.1m E; P.O., G,L,M 6.6m W)	RGLMw	63.6	
		103.4	Partnership Shelter	Sw	63.4	
		107.3	Va. 601	R	59.5	
		111.1	Va. 670 (Teas Road),			
			South Fork Holston River (2,450')	R	55.7	
		112.0	Va. 672	R	54.8	
		113.2	Trimpi Shelter	Sw	53.6	
		115.3	High Point (4,040')		51.5	
		115.8	Bobby's Trail, Raccoon Branch Campground			
			(C,w 0.2m E; 3.3m E)	Cw	51.0	

Left vertical labels: Piedmont A.T. Hikers / *Va. Section 40* / *Mt. Rogers A.T. Club* / *Va. Section 41*

Right vertical label: SW Va. Map 3

Southwest Virginia

Club	GBS	N to S	Features	Facilities (see page 14 for codes)	S to N	Map
			Miles from New River, VA		*Miles from Damascus, VA*	
		117.3	Dickey Gap, Va. 16, Va. 650; **Troutdale, Va., P.O. 24378** (P.O. 2.7m E; L 2.3m E)	RL	49.5	
		118.5	Comers Creek, Comers Creek Falls Trail (3,200')	w	48.3	
		118.9	Dickey Gap Trail	Cw	47.9	
		121.0	Stream	w	45.8	
		121.8	Hurricane Creek Trail		45.0	
		122.4	Hurricane Mountain Shelter	Sw	44.4	
		123.3	Chestnut Flats, Iron Mountain Trail		43.5	
		123.6	Hurricane Mountain (4,320'), Tennessee-New River Divide		43.2	
		125.6	Va. 603, Fox Creek (3,480')	Rw	41.2	
		127.3	Old Orchard Shelter	Sw	39.5	
		128.9	Pine Mountain Trail (5,000')		37.9	
		130.3	The Scales		36.5	
		130.7	Stone Mountain		36.1	
		133.0	Wilson Creek Trail (Cw 1.3m E)	Cw	33.8	
		133.2	Big Wilson Creek	Cw	33.6	
		133.3	Grayson Highlands State Park, Wise Shelter (4,460')	Sw	33.5	
		135.4	Park service road to Massie Gap		31.4	
		136.2	Wilburn Ridge		30.6	
		137.4	Rhododendron Gap (5,440')		29.4	
		138.4	Thomas Knob Shelter	Sw	28.4	
		138.6	Mt. Rogers Spur Trail		28.2	
		140.6	Deep Gap (w 0.2m E)	w	26.2	
		142.6	Va. 600, Elk Garden (4,434')	R	24.2	
		145.0	Whitetop Mountain Road (USFS 89)	R	21.8	

Mt. Rogers A.T. Club

Va. Section 42

Va. Section 43

SW Va. Map 3

SW Va. Map 4

Southwest Virginia

		Miles from New River, VA		*Miles from Damascus, VA*	

Club	GBS	NtoS	Features	Facilities	StoN	Map
	Va. Sec. 44	145.1	Spring	W	21.7	
		145.9	Buzzard Rock (5,080'),			
			Whitetop Mountain		20.9	
		148.4	Va. 601 (Beech Mountain Road)	Rw	18.4	
		149.7	U.S. 58 (3,160'); Summit Cut, Va.	R	17.1	
Mt. Rogers A.T. Club (MRATC)		150.8	Lost Mountain Shelter	Sw	16.0	
		152.0	Va. 859 (Grassy Ridge Road)	R	14.8	
		152.6	Virginia Creeper Trail,			
			Whitetop Laurel Creek		14.2	
		153.2	Va. 728, Creek Junction (2,720')			
			(R 0.5m E)	R	13.6	SW Va. Map 4
		155.0	Bear Tree Gap side trail (C 0.6m W)	C	11.8	
	Va. Section 45	157.3	Saunders Shelter			
			(S,w 0.2m W)	Sw	9.5	
		157.6	Straight Mountain (3,500')		9.2	
		159.2	Taylors Valley Side Trail			
			(M 0.6m E)	M	7.6	
		159.8	Stream	W	7.0	
		161.2	U.S. 58, Straight Branch,			
			Feathercamp Branch (2,200'),			
			Feathercamp Trail	Rw	5.6	
		161.8	Beech Grove Trail		5.0	
		163.3	Feathercamp Ridge,			
			Iron Mountain Trail (2,850')		3.5	
		165.8	U.S. 58, Va. 91, Virginia Creeper Trail	R	1.0	
		166.8	**Damascus, Va., P.O. 24236** (1,928')	★		
			(P.O.,G,L,M on A.T.)	RGLM	0.0	

Tennessee–North Carolina

Club	GBS	N to S	Features	Facilities (see page 14 for codes)	S to N	Map
		Miles from Damascus, VA			*Miles from Fontana Dam, NC*	
		0.0	**Damascus, Va., P.O. 24236** (1,928')	★		
			(P.O.,G,L,M on A.T.)	RGLM	304.0	
		2.1	Campsite	Cw	301.9	
		3.7	Virginia–Tennessee Line		300.3	
		4.8	Backbone Rock Trail		299.2	
		10.2	Abingdon Gap Shelter (3,785')	CSw	293.8	
		11.3	McQueens Gap, USFS 69	R	292.7	
		11.7	McQueens Knob		292.3	
		13.1	Double Spring Gap	Cw	290.9	
		15.0	Low Gap, U.S. 421 (3,384'); **Shady Valley, Tenn., P.O. 37688** (w on A.T.; P.O.,G,M 3m E)	RGMw	289.0	
		18.5	Double Springs Shelter, Holston Mountain Trail (4,080')	CSw	285.5	
		19.4	Campsite (north of Osborne Farm)	Cw	284.6	
		21.5	Tenn. 91 (3,450')	R	282.5	
		22.4	Stream	w	281.6	
		24.8	Spring	w	279.2	
		24.9	Nick Grindstaff Monument		279.1	
		26.2	Iron Mountain Shelter (4,125')	CS(nw)	277.8	
		26.4	Spring	w	277.6	
		27.8	Turkeypen Gap		276.2	
		28.2	Big Laurel Branch Wilderness (north end)		275.8	
		29.2	Campsite at boggy spring	Cw	274.8	
		33.0	Vandeventer Shelter (3,510') (C,S on A.T.; w 0.5m W)	CSw	271.0	
		34.7	Spring	w	269.3	
		37.7	Wilbur Dam Road	R	266.3	
		39.0	Watauga Dam (north end)		265.0	

Side labels: MRATC · Tenn.–N.C. Section 1 · Tenn.–N.C. Section 2 · Green Mountain Club · Tenn.–N.C. Section 3 · Tenn.–N.C. Map 1

Tennessee–North Carolina

Club	GBS	N to S	Features	Facilities (see page 14 for codes)	S to N	Map
		Miles from Damascus, VA			*Miles from Fontana Dam, NC*	
		40.2	Stream (2,100')	w	263.8	
		40.6	Griffith Branch	w	263.4	
		42.1	U.S. 321;			
			Hampton, Tenn., P.O. 37658			
			(P.O.,G,M 2.6m W; G,L 1.8m W)	RGLM	261.9	
		42.6	Campsite south of Pond Mtn. Wilderness	C(nw)	261.4	
		45.2	Pond Flats	Cw	258.8	
		48.0	Hampton Blueline Trail to U.S. 321	w	256.0	
		48.5	Waycaster Spring	w	255.5	
		48.8	Laurel Fork Shelter (2,400')	Sw	255.2	
		49.5	Laurel Fork Falls	w	254.5	
		50.7	Dennis Cove, USFS 50			
			(C,G,L,M 0.5m E; C,L 0.2m W)	RCGLMw	253.3	
		52.4	Side trail to Coon Den Falls		251.6	
		54.9	Canute Place	Cw	249.1	
		55.8	Tower Road, White Rocks Mountain (4,206')	R	248.2	
		57.0	Moreland Gap	Cw	247.0	
		60.1	Hardcore Cascades	w	243.9	
		62.8	Laurel Fork	w	241.2	
		63.8	Stream	w	240.2	
		65.0	Walnut Mountain Road	R	239.0	
		65.8	Campsite south of Slide Hollow	Cw	238.2	
		66.6	Mountaineer Falls Shelter	Sw	237.4	
		66.8	Mountaineer Falls Campsite	Cw	237.2	
		69.2	Campsite along Elk River	Cw	234.8	
		71.8	Campbell Hollow Road	R	232.2	
		72.1	Buck Mountain Road	R	231.9	
		75.2	Bear Branch Road	R	228.8	

Left margin labels: *Tennessee Eastman Hiking Club* — Tenn.–N.C. Section 4 — Tenn.–N.C. Section 5

Right margin labels: Tenn.–N.C. Map 1 — Tenn.–N.C. Map 2

Tennessee–North Carolina

Miles from Damascus, VA

Miles from Fontana Dam, NC

Club	GBS	N to S	Features	Facilities	S to N	Map
		75.4	U.S. 19E (2,895'); **Roan Mountain, Tenn., P.O. 37687;** ★ **Elk Park, N.C., P.O. 28622** (P.O.,G,M 3.4m W; P.O. 2.5m E; C 4.0m E; G 1.2m E; L 3m E; M 0.5m E, 1m E)	RCGLM	228.6	
		76.0	Apple House Campsite	Cw	228.0	
		76.1	Wilder Mine Hollow Group Campsite	Cw	227.9	
		78.4	Doll Flats	Cw	225.6	
		80.8	Hump Mountain (5,587')		223.2	
		81.7	Bradley Gap	Cw	222.3	
		83.0	Little Hump Mountain (5,459')	Cw	221.0	
		84.6	Yellow Mountain Gap (4,682') (w 0.2m E; C 0.3m E)	Cw	219.4	
		86.5	Stan Murray Shelter (5,050')	CSw	217.5	
		88.3	Side trail to Grassy Ridge		215.7	
		90.2	Carvers Gap, Tenn. 143, N.C. 261 (5,512')	Rw	213.8	
		93.8	Ash Gap	Cw	210.2	
		96.8	Hughes Gap (4,040') (G 3.2m W; C,L 2m E)	RCGL	207.2	
		99.0	Little Rock Knob (4,918')	C(nw)	205.0	
		100.2	Clyde Smith Shelter	CSw	203.8	
		101.3	Campsite at row of maple trees	Cw	202.7	
		102.1	Greasy Creek Gap (4,034') (C,w 0.2m W; L 0.7m E)	CLw	201.9	
		105.0	Orchard Campsite	Cw	199.0	
		106.2	Iron Mountain Gap, Tenn. 107, N.C. 226 (3,723') (G 4.7m W)	RG	197.8	
		109.3	Cherry Gap Shelter	CSw	194.7	
		110.4	Low Gap (3,900')	w	193.6	

Left margin (vertical labels): *Tennessee Eastman Hiking Club* — Tenn.–N.C. Section 6 — Sec. 7 — Tenn.–N.C. Section 8 — Sec. 9

Right margin (vertical labels): Tenn.–N.C. Map 2

Tennessee–North Carolina

Club	GBS	N to S	Features	Facilities (see page 14 for codes)	S to N	Map
			Miles from Damascus, VA	*Miles from Fontana Dam, NC*		
		112.6	Unaka Mountain (5,180')		191.4	
		113.6	USFS 230	R	190.4	
		114.2	Beauty Spot Gap (4,100')	RCw	189.8	Tenn.–N.C. Map 2
		115.5	Spring	Rw	188.5	
		115.8	Beauty Spot	RC(nw)	188.2	
		117.0	USFS 230	R	187.0	
	Tenn.–N.C. Section 9	118.1	Indian Grave Gap, Tenn. 395 (C 3.3m W)	RC	185.9	
		120.9	Spring	w	183.1	
Tennessee Eastman Hiking Club		122.2	Curley Maple Gap Shelter (3,070')	CSw	181.8	
	Tenn.–N.C. Section 10	125.1	Nolichucky River Valley (C,L,M on A.T.)	RCLM	178.9	
		126.4	Nolichucky River (1,700'); **Erwin, Tenn., P.O. 37650** (P.O.,G,M 3.8m W; L 1.2m W; G,L 2.3m W)	★ RGLM	177.6	
		130.3	Temple Hill Gap (2,850')		173.7	
		132.7	No Business Knob Shelter	CSw	171.3	Tenn.–N.C. Map 3
		132.9	Spring	w	171.1	
		135.3	Devils Creek Gap (3,400')	R	168.7	
		137.0	Oglesby Branch	w	167.0	
		137.6	Spivey Gap, U.S. 19W (3,200')	Rw	166.4	
		138.1	Campsite	Cw	165.9	
Carolina Mtn. Club	Tenn.–N.C. Section 11	139.6	Trail to High Rocks (4,100')		164.4	
		139.9	Whistling Gap	Cw	164.1	
		141.9	Little Bald		162.1	
		142.9	Campsite	Cw	161.1	
		143.3	Bald Mountain Shelter	Sw	160.7	
		144.2	Big Stamp (C,w 0.3m W; M 1.5m E)	CMw	159.8	

Tennessee–North Carolina

Club	GBS	N to S	Features	Facilities (see page 14 for codes)	S to N	Map
		Miles from Damascus, VA			*Miles from Fontana Dam, NC*	
		144.5	Big Bald (5,516')		159.5	
		145.3	Spring	w	158.7	
		147.3	Low Gap	w	156.7	
		148.7	Street Gap (4,100')		155.3	
		150.3	Springs	w	153.7	
		151.0	Sams Gap, U.S. 23, I-26 (3,800') (M 1.9m E, 2.8m E; G 3.2m E)	RGM	153.0	
		152.8	High Rock (4,460')		151.2	
		153.4	Hogback Ridge Shelter (C,S 0.1m E; w 0.3m E)	CSw	150.6	
		154.6	Rice Gap (3,800')		149.4	
		155.6	Big Flat	C	148.4	
		156.2	Frozen Knob (4,579')		147.8	
		159.0	Rector Laurel Road (2,960')	R	145.0	
		159.5	Devil Fork Gap, N.C. 212	R	144.5	
		161.3	Campsite	Cw	142.7	
		162.2	Flint Mountain Shelter (3,550')	CSw	141.8	
		163.8	Spring	w	140.2	
		167.0	Big Butt (4,750')	C	137.0	
		168.9	Jerry Cabin Shelter (4,150')	CSw	135.1	
		171.4	Big Firescald Knob	w	132.6	
		172.4	Blackstack Cliffs (0.1m W)		131.6	
		172.6	White Rock Cliffs (0.1m E)		131.4	
		172.7	Spring	w	131.3	
		174.4	Camp Creek Bald, side trail to fire tower (4,750')	R	129.6	
		176.2	Little Laurel Shelter (3,300')	CSw	127.8	
		181.1	Allen Gap, N.C. 208, Tenn. 70 (2,234')	Rw	122.9	
		183.3	Spring	w	120.7	
		184.8	Spring Mountain Shelter (3,300')	CSw	119.2	

Carolina Mountain Club

Tenn.–N.C. Sec. 11 · Tenn.–N.C. Section 12 · Tenn.–N.C. Section 13

Tenn.–N.C. Map 3

Tennessee–North Carolina

Club	GBS	N to S	Features	Facilities (see page 14 for codes)	S to N	Map
			Miles from *Damascus, VA*		*Miles from* *Fontana Dam, NC*	
		186.5	Hurricane Gap	R	117.5	
		187.6	Rich Mountain Fire Tower Side Trail (3,600')	Cw	116.4	
		189.9	Tanyard Gap, U.S. 25 & 70 (2,278')	R	114.1	
		192.5	Pump Gap		111.5	
		194.4	Lovers Leap Rock		109.6	
		195.8	U.S. 25 & 70, N.C. 209 (1,326'); **Hot Springs, N.C., P.O. 28743** (P.O.,C,G,L,M on A.T.)	★ RCGLM	108.2	
		199.0	Deer Park Mountain Shelter	CSw	105.0	
		202.4	Garenflo Gap (2,500')	R	101.6	
		204.9	Big Rock Spring	w	99.1	
		206.5	Bluff Mountain (4,686')		97.5	
		208.9	Walnut Mountain Shelter (C 0.1m W)	CSw	95.1	
		210.2	Lemon Gap, N.C. 1182, Tenn. 107 (3,550')	R	93.8	
		213.7	Roaring Fork Shelter	CSw	90.3	
		215.6	Max Patch Summit (4,629')		88.4	
		216.4	Max Patch Road (N.C. 1182)	R	87.6	
		219.1	Brown Gap	Rw	84.9	
		222.0	Deep Gap, Groundhog Creek Shelter (2,900') (C,S,w 0.2m E)	CSw	82.0	
		224.0	Campsite	Cw	80.0	
		224.5	Snowbird Mountain (4,263')	R	79.5	
		226.0	Spanish Oak Gap		78.0	
		226.9	Painter Branch	Cw	77.1	
		229.2	Green Corner Road (C,G,L 0.2m W)	RCGL	74.8	
		229.7	I-40	R	74.3	

Left margin labels: Carolina Mountain Club; Tenn.–N.C. Sec. 14; Tenn.–N.C. Section 15; Tenn.–N.C. Section 16

Right margin label: Tenn.–N.C. Map 4

Tennessee–North Carolina

Club	GBS	N to S	Features	Facilities (see page 14 for codes)	S to N	Map
			Miles from Damascus, VA		*Miles from Fontana Dam, NC*	
Carolina Mtn. Club		230.1	Pigeon River (1,400')		73.9	Tenn.–N.C. Map 4
		230.3	State Line Branch	Cw	73.7	
		231.6	Davenport Gap, Tenn. 32, S.R. 1397; eastern boundary, Great Smoky Mountains National Park (1,975') (C 2.5m E)	RC	72.4	
Smoky Mountains Hiking Club	Tenn.–N.C. Section 17 (N.C. 1)	232.7	Davenport Gap Shelter	Sw	71.3	Great Smoky Mtns. N.P. Map
		234.9	Spring	w	69.1	
		236.4	Spring	w	67.6	
		236.8	Mt. Cammerer Side Trail (5,000')		67.2	
		238.9	Low Gap Trail		65.1	
		239.6	Cosby Knob Shelter	Sw	64.4	
		240.0	Cosby Knob		64.0	
		243.3	Snake Den Ridge Trail		60.7	
		245.3	Guyot Spring	w	58.7	
		245.9	Guyot Spur (6,360')		58.1	
		247.3	Tri-Corner Knob Shelter, Balsam Mtn. Trail	Sw	56.7	
		248.4	Mt. Chapman		55.6	
		250.1	Mt. Sequoyah		53.9	
		252.5	Hughes Ridge Trail to Pecks Corner Shelter (w on A.T.; S,w 0.5m E)	Sw	51.5	
		254.5	Bradleys View		49.5	
		257.6	Porters Gap, The Sawteeth		46.4	
		259.0	Charlies Bunion		45.0	
		259.9	Icewater Spring Shelter	Sw	44.1	
		260.2	Boulevard Trail to Mt. LeConte		43.8	
		263.0	Newfound Gap, U.S. 441 (5,045')	Rw	41.0	
		264.7	Indian Gap, Road Prong Trail	R	39.3	
		266.1	Spring	w	37.9	

Tennessee–North Carolina

Club	GBS	N to S	Features	Facilities (see page 14 for codes)	S to N	Map
			Miles from Damascus, VA	*Miles from Fontana Dam, NC*		
		267.9	Sugarland Mtn. Trail to Mt. Collins Shelter (5,900') (S,w 0.5m W)	Sw	36.1	
		270.2	Mt. Love		33.8	
		270.7	*Kuwohi* (Clingmans Dome) (6,643') (R,w 0.5m E)	Rw	33.3	
		273.5	Double Spring Gap Shelter (5,507')	Sw	30.5	
		275.0	Silers Bald		29.0	
		275.2	Silers Bald Shelter	Sw	28.8	
		278.2	Buckeye Gap (4,817'), Miry Ridge Trail	w	25.8	
		280.6	Sams Gap, Greenbrier Ridge Trail	w	23.4	
		280.9	Derrick Knob Shelter	Sw	23.1	
		281.9	Sugar Tree Gap (4,435')		22.1	
		283.6	Mineral Gap (5,030')		20.4	
		284.2	Beechnut Gap	w	19.8	
		285.3	Thunderhead, east peak (5,527')		18.7	
		285.9	Rocky Top		18.1	
		287.0	Eagle Creek Trail to Spence Field Shelter, Bote Mountain Trail (S,w 0.2m E)	Sw	17.0	
		289.9	Russell Field Shelter	Sw	14.1	
		291.4	Little Abrams Gap (4,120')		12.6	
		292.5	Devils Tater Patch (4,775')		11.5	
		293.0	Mollies Ridge Shelter	Sw	11.0	
		294.7	Ekaneetlee Gap (3,842')	w	9.3	
		296.2	Doe Knob (4,520'), Gregory Bald Trail		7.8	
		298.4	Birch Spring Gap; Campsite #113	Cw	5.6	
		299.7	Shuckstack fire tower (0.1m E)		4.3	
		304.0	Little Tennessee River, Fontana Dam; southern boundary, Great Smoky Mountains National Park (1,800')	R	0.0	

Smoky Mountains Hiking Club

Tenn.–N.C. Section 18 (N.C. 2)

Great Smoky Mtns. N.P. Map

Club	GBS	N to S	Features	Facilities (see page 14 for codes)		S to N	Map

Miles from Fontana Dam, NC

Miles from Springer Mountain, GA

		0.0	Little Tennessee River, Fontana Dam; southern boundary, Great Smoky Mountains National Park (1,740')	R	167.0	
		0.4	Fontana Dam Visitor Center	Rw	166.6	
		0.8	"Fontana Hilton" Shelter	CSw	166.2	
		2.1	N.C. 28; Fontana Marina			
			Fontana Dam, N.C., P.O. 28733	★		
			(P.O.,G,L,M 1.8m W)	RGLM	164.9	
		4.4	Campsite	Cw	162.6	
		4.8	Walker Gap (3,450')		162.2	
		6.2	Black Gum Gap		160.8	
		7.6	Cable Gap Shelter	CSw	159.4	
		8.5	Yellow Creek Gap, S.R. 1242 (2,980') (Yellow Creek Mountain Road) (L 4m E)	RL	158.5	
		10.9	Cody Gap	Cw	156.1	
		11.7	Hogback Gap		155.3	
		13.5	Brown Fork Gap	w	153.5	
		13.9	Brown Fork Gap Shelter	Sw	153.1	
		15.3	Sweetwater Gap		151.7	
		16.3	Stecoah Gap, N.C. 143 (3,165') (Sweetwater Creek Road)	Rw	150.7	
		18.4	Simp Gap		148.6	
		19.4	Locust Cove Gap	Cw	147.6	
		21.8	Cheoah Bald (5,062')		145.2	
		23.0	Sassafras Gap Shelter	CSw	144.0	
		23.9	Swim Bald		143.1	
		27.0	Grassy Gap (3,050')		140.0	
		28.5	Wright Gap	R	138.5	

Left margin labels (top to bottom): *Smoky Mountains Hiking Club* — N.C. Section 3, N.C. Section 4, N.C. Section 5

Right margin label: N.C.–Ga. Map 1

North Carolina–Georgia

			Miles from Fontana Dam, NC		*Miles from Springer Mountain, GA*	
		30.1	U.S. 19, U.S. 74, Nantahala River (1,723');			
			Wesser, N.C. (L,M on A.T.; G 1m E)	RGLM	136.9	
		30.9	A. Rufus Morgan Shelter	CSw	136.1	
		34.0	Jump-up Lookout (4,000')		133.0	
		35.8	Wesser Creek Trail, Wesser Bald Shelter	CS	131.2	
		35.9	Spring	w	131.1	
		36.6	Wesser Bald (4,627'), viewing tower (0.1m E)		130.4	
		38.0	Tellico Gap, S.R. 1365 (3,850')	R	129.0	
		39.4	Big Branch Campsite	Cw	127.6	
		39.7	Side trail to Rocky Bald Lookout		127.3	
		40.9	Copper Ridge Bald Lookout (5,080')		126.1	
		41.6	Cold Spring Shelter	CSw	125.4	
		42.8	Burningtown Gap, S.R. 1397 (4,236')	R	124.2	
		45.1	Licklog Gap			
			(C 0.1 W, w 0.3m W)	Cw	121.9	
		46.4	Wayah Shelter	CSw	120.6	
		46.9	Campsite	Cw	120.1	
		47.3	Wayah Bald (5,342')	R	119.7	
		49.2	Wine Spring	Cw	117.8	
		49.7	USFS 69	Rw	117.3	
		51.5	Wayah Gap, S.R. 1310 (4,180')	R	115.5	
		53.2	Siler Bald Shelter (4,700')			
			(C,S,w 0.5m E)	CSw	113.8	
		55.4	Panther Gap		111.6	
		56.3	Swinging Lick Gap		110.7	
		56.5	Moore Creek Campsite	Cw	110.5	
		57.4	Winding Stair Gap, U.S. 64;			
			Franklin, N.C., P.O. 28734	★		
			(w on A.T.; P.O.,G,L,M 10m E)	RGLMw	109.6	

Club labels (left margin): Nantahala Hiking Club — N.C. Section 6, N.C. Section 7, N.C. Section 8

Map labels (right margin): N.C.–Ga. Map 2

North Carolina–Georgia

Club	GBS	N to S	Features	Facilities (see page 14 for codes)	S to N	Map
			Miles from Fontana Dam, NC	*Miles from Springer Mountain, GA*		
		60.5	Wallace Gap, "Old 64" (3,738')	R	106.5	
		61.1	Rock Gap, Standing Indian Campground (C 1.5m W)	RC	105.9	
		61.2	Rock Gap Shelter	CSw	105.8	
		63.7	Glassmine Gap		103.3	
		64.6	Long Branch Shelter	CSw	102.4	
		67.1	Albert Mountain (5,250')		99.9	
	N.C. Section 9	67.4	Bearpen Trail, USFS 67	R	99.6	
		68.4	Spring	w	98.6	
		68.7	Mooney Gap, USFS 83	R	98.3	
Nantahala Hiking Club		69.6	Betty Creek Gap (4,300')	Cw	97.4	N.C.–Ga. Map 2
		73.3	Carter Gap Shelter	CSw	93.7	
		73.7	Timber Ridge Trail		93.3	
		76.5	Beech Gap (4,460')	Cw	90.5	
		79.4	Lower Ridge Trail, Standing Indian Mountain (5,498') (w 0.2m W)	w	87.6	
		80.9	Standing Indian Shelter	CSw	86.1	
		81.8	Deep Gap, USFS 71 (4,341') (C 0.1m W)	CRw	85.2	
	N.C. Section 10	83.9	Wateroak Gap		83.1	
		84.8	Chunky Gal Trail		82.2	
		85.0	Whiteoak Stamp	Cw	82.0	
		85.8	Muskrat Creek Shelter (4,600')	CSw	81.2	
		86.7	Sassafras Gap		80.3	
		88.6	Bly Gap (3,840')	Cw	78.4	
		88.7	North Carolina–Georgia Line		78.3	
GA. A.T. Club	Ga. Section 11	90.6	Rich Cove Gap		76.4	N.C.–Ga. Map 3
		90.8	Spring	w	76.2	
		91.8	Blue Ridge Gap (3,020')		75.2	
		92.4	As Knob		74.6	

North Carolina–Georgia

Club	GBS	N to S	Features	Facilities (see page 14 for codes)	S to N	Map
			Miles from Fontana Dam, NC	*Miles from Springer Mountain, GA*		
	Ga. Section 11	93.1	Plumorchard Gap Shelter (C,S,w 0.2m E)	CSw	73.9	
		94.3	Bull Gap (3,550')		72.7	
		95.8	Cowart Gap		71.2	
		96.5	Little Bald Knob Campsite	Cw	70.5	
		97.6	Dicks Creek Gap, U.S. 76 (2,675');			
			Hiawassee, Ga., P.O. 30546	★		
			(w on A.T.; L 3.5m W;			
			P.O.,G,L,M 11m W)	RGLMw	69.4	
Georgia A.T. Club		98.2	Streams	w	68.8	N.C.–Ga. Map 3
		98.8	Moreland Gap		68.2	
		99.8	Powell Mountain (3,850')		67.2	
		100.0	McClure Gap	C	67.0	
	Ga. Section 12	101.2	Deep Gap Shelter (3,550') (C,S,w 0.3m E)	CSw	65.8	
		102.0	Kelly Knob (4,276')		65.0	
		103.0	Addis Gap (3,304') (C,w 0.5m E)	Cw	64.0	
		103.9	Sassafras Gap	w	63.1	
		105.0	Swag of the Blue Ridge		62.0	
		108.6	Tray Mountain Shelter (C,S 0.2m W; w 0.3m W)	CSw	58.4	
		109.1	Tray Mountain (4,430')		57.9	
		109.9	Tray Gap, Tray Mountain Road (USFS 79/698)	R	57.1	
		110.6	Cheese Factory Site	Cw	56.4	
		110.9	Tray Mountain Road (USFS 79)	R	56.1	
		111.6	Indian Grave Gap, USFS 283 (3,113')	R	55.4	
		112.9	Rocky Mountain (4,017')	C	54.1	
		113.7	Stream	w	53.3	

North Carolina–Georgia

Club	GBS	N to S	Features	Facilities (see page 14 for codes)	S to N	Map
			Miles from Fontana Dam, NC	*Miles from Springer Mountain, GA*		
		114.3	Unicoi Gap, Ga. 75 (2,949');			
			Helen, Ga., P.O. 30545	★		
			(P.O.,G,L,M 9m E; C,G,L,M 3.8m W)	RCGLM	52.7	
		115.8	Blue Mountain (4,025')		51.2	
		116.7	Blue Mountain Shelter	CSw	50.3	
		117.4	Spring	w	49.6	
		117.6	Spaniards Knob Campsite	C	49.4	
		118.3	Red Clay Gap		48.7	
		119.0	Chattahoochee Gap (3,500')	w	48.0	
		120.2	Cold Springs Gap		46.8	
		122.6	Poplar Stamp Gap	Cw	44.4	
		124.0	Low Gap Shelter (3,050')	CSw	43.0	
		124.8	Sheep Rock Top		42.2	
		126.7	Poor Mountain		40.3	
		127.9	White Oak Stamp		39.1	
		128.8	Hogpen Gap, Ga. 348 (3,450')	Rw	38.2	
		129.0	Whitley Gap Shelter			
			(S 1.2m E; w 1.5m E)	Sw	38.0	
		129.7	Tesnatee Gap, Ga. 348 (3,138')	R	37.3	
		130.7	Cowrock Mountain (3,842')		36.3	
		131.5	Baggs Creek Gap	Cw	35.5	
		132.0	Wolf Laurel Top		35.0	
		132.7	Rock Spring Top	w	34.3	
		133.5	Swaim Gap		33.5	
		134.2	Levelland Mountain (3,942')		32.8	
		134.6	Bull Gap	Cw	32.4	
		135.7	Neel Gap, U.S. 19/129 (3,125')	★		
			(G,L on A.T.; L 0.3m E;			
			C,G 3m W; C,L 3.5m W)	RCGLw	31.3	

Georgia A.T. Club — Ga. Section 13, Ga. Section 14

N.C.–Ga. Map 3

North Carolina–Georgia

Miles from Fontana Dam, NC

Miles from Springer Mountain, GA

Club	GBS	N to S	Features	Facilities	S to N	Map
		136.7	Flatrock Gap, Trail to Byron Reece Memorial (w 0.2m W)	w	30.3	
		138.1	Blood Mountain Shelter (4,461')	S(nw)	28.9	
		138.9	Blood Mountain Campsites	Cw	28.1	
		139.0	Slaughter Creek Trail	w	28.0	
	Ga. Section 15	139.3	Bird Gap (3,650'), Woods Hole Shelter (S,w 0.5m W)	CSw	27.7	
		140.7	Jarrard Gap (3,250') (w 0.3m W; w 1m W, G,L 2m W)	GLw	26.3	
		141.3	Burnett Field Mountain		25.7	
		143.0	Lance Creek Campsite	Cw	24.0	
		144.1	Dan Gap		22.9	
		145.1	Big Cedar Mountain (3,737')		21.9	
Georgia A.T. Club		146.5	Woody Gap, Ga. 60 (3,173'); **Suches, Ga., P.O. 30572** (w 0.1m W; P.O.,C,G 2m W)	★ RCGw	20.5	N.C.–Ga. Map 4
	Ga. Section 16	148.0	Ramrock Mountain		19.0	
		150.1	Gooch Gap, USFS 42 (2,821')	Rw	16.9	
		151.3	Gooch Mountain Shelter (C,S,w 0.1m W)	CSw	15.7	
		152.8	Justus Creek (2,550')	Cw	14.2	
		154.8	Cooper Gap, USFS 42/80	R	12.2	
		156.5	Horse Gap (2,673')	R	10.5	
		158.4	Hightower Gap, USFS 42/69 (2,854')	R	8.6	
	Ga. Section 17	158.9	Hawk Mountain Shelter (S 0.2m W; w 0.4m W)	Sw	8.1	
		159.6	Hawk Mountain Campsite	Cw	7.4	
		160.8	USFS 251	R	6.2	
		161.8	Side trail to Long Creek Falls, junction with Benton MacKaye and Duncan Ridge trails		5.2	

North Carolina–Georgia

Club	GBS	N to S	Features	Facilities (see page 14 for codes)	S to N	Map
		Miles from Fontana Dam, NC		*Miles from Springer Mountain, GA*		
		162.7	Three Forks, USFS 58 (2,530')	RCw	4.3	
		162.8	Benton MacKaye Trail		4.2	
		163.2	Stover Creek	w	3.8	
		164.1	Stover Creek	w	2.9	
Georgia A.T. Club	*Ga. Section 17*	164.2	Stover Creek Shelter (C,S,w 0.2m E)	CSw	2.8	*N.C.–Ga. Map 4*
		165.1	Benton MacKaye Trail		1.9	
		166.0	USFS 42	R	1.0	
		166.7	Southern terminus, Benton MacKaye Trail		0.3	
		166.8	Springer Mountain Shelter (C,S,w 0.2m E)	CSw	0.2	
		167.0	Springer Mountain (3,782')		0.0	

Amicalola Falls Approach Trail

Club	GBS	N to S	Features	Facilities (see page 14 for codes)	S to N	Map
			Miles from Springer Mountain, GA	*Miles from Amicalola Falls State Park*		
		0.0	Springer Mountain (3,782')		8.8	
		1.5	Black Gap Shelter (temporarily closed)	Cw	7.3	
		2.8	Nimblewill Gap, USFS 28 (3,100')	R	6.0	
		3.4	Side trail to Len Foote Hike Inn (L,M,w 1m E)	LMw	5.4	
Georgia A.T. Club	Approach Trail	3.7	Frosty Mountain Road (USFS 46)	R	5.1	N.C.–Ga. Map 4
		4.0	Frosty Mountain (3,382')	Cw	4.8	
		5.6	High Shoals Road	R	3.2	
		7.3	USFS 46	R	1.5	
		7.4	Side trail to Len Foote Hike Inn (L,M,w 5m E)	LMw	1.4	
		7.6	Amicalola Lodge Road (L,M,w 0.2m E)	RLMw	1.2	
		8.8	Visitors Center, Amicalola Falls State Park (1,700')	RCSw	0.0	

A.T. Maintaining Clubs

Maine A.T. Club	www.matc.org
Appalachian Mountain Club	www.outdoors.org
Randolph Mountain Club	www.randolphmountainclub.org
Dartmouth Outing Club	www.outdoors.dartmouth.edu
Green Mountain Club	www.greenmountainclub.org
AMC Western Massachusetts Chapter	www.amc-wma.org
AMC Connecticut Chapter	www.ct-amc.org
New York–New Jersey Trail Conference	www.nynjtc.org
Batona Hiking Club	www.batona.wildapricot.org
AMC Delaware Valley Chapter	www.amcdv.org
Keystone Trails Association	www.kta-hike.org
Blue Mountain Eagle Climbing Club	www.bmecc.org
Allentown Hiking Club	www.allentownhikingclub.org
Susquehanna A.T. Club	www.satc-hike.org
York Hiking Club	www.yorkhikingclub.com
Cumberland Valley A.T. Club	www.cvatclub.org
Mountain Club of Maryland	www.mcomd.org
Potomac A.T. Club	www.patc.net
Old Dominion A.T. Club	www.odatc.net
Tidewater A.T. Club	www.tidewateratc.com
Natural Bridge A.T. Club	www.nbatc.org
Roanoke A.T. Club	www.ratc.org
Outdoor Club of Virginia Tech	www.outdoor.org.vt.edu
Piedmont A.T. Hikers	www.path-at.org
Mount Rogers A.T. Club	www.mratc.org
Tennessee Eastman Hiking Club	www.tehcc.org
Carolina Mountain Club	www.carolinamountainclub.org
Smoky Mountains Hiking Club	www.smhclub.org
Nantahala Hiking Club	www.nantahalahikingclub.org
Georgia A.T. Club	www.georgia-atclub.org

History of the Appalachian Trail *Data Book*

The model for the *Appalachian Trail Data Book* was the "Mileage Fact Sheet" compiled by Ed Garvey and Gus Crews, published simultaneously in 1971 by the then-Appalachian Trail Conference and Appalachian Books (Oakton, Virginia) as an appendix to the late Mr. Garvey's *Appalachian Hiker*.

The first edition (1977) of the *Appalachian Trail Data Book* was compiled by the late Raymond F. Hunt of Kingsport, Tennessee, who continued to perform this volunteer service annually until 1983, when he began a six-year term as chair of the ATC.

The editions since then have been compiled by Daniel D. Chazin of Teaneck, New Jersey, an active volunteer with the New York–New Jersey Trail Conference and editor of the *Appalachian Trail Guide to New York–New Jersey*. Mr. Chazin draws each fall on the work of editors and data compilers of the other ten guidebooks, thirty maintaining clubs, and Conservancy regional offices for updated information on each section of the Appalachian Trail.

The Appalachian Trail Community™ Network

The Appalachian Trail Community™ program is an ATC initiative that seeks to develop mutually beneficial relationships with interested towns and counties along the Trail—to enhance their economies, further protect the Trail, and engage a new generation of volunteers.

Communities designated as of November 2024:

Kingfield, ME	Bland, VA
Millinocket, ME	Bluemont, VA
Monson, ME	Buena Vista, VA
Rangeley, ME	Damascus, VA
Gorham, NH	Elkton, VA
Hanover, NH	Front Royal/Warren County, VA
Bennington, VT	Glasgow, VA
Manchester, VT	Harrisonburg, VA
Norwich, VT	Hillsboro, VA
Cheshire, MA	Luray/Page County, VA
Dalton, MA	Marion/Smyth County, VA
Great Barrington, MA	Narrows, VA
Lee, MA	Nelson County, VA
North Adams, MA	Pearisburg, VA
Harlem Valley (Dover and Pawling), NY	Troutville, VA
Warwick, NY	Round Hill, VA
Greater Blairstown, NJ	Waynesboro, VA
Vernon, NJ	Roan Mountain, TN
Boiling Springs, PA	Unicoi County, TN
Delaware Water Gap, PA	Fontana Dam, NC
Duncannon, PA	Franklin, NC
Greater Waynesboro, PA	Hot Springs, NC
Wind Gap, PA	Blairsville/Union County, GA
Boonsboro, MD	Clayton/Rabun County, GA
Brunswick, MD	Dahlonega, GA
Harpers Ferry/Bolivar, WV	Ellijay/Gilmer County, GA
Abingdon, VA	Hiawassee/Towns County, GA
Berryville/Clarke County, VA	Helen/White County, GA

Those listed in the *Data Book* are indicated by a ★ in the Facilities column.

MOUNTAINEERS BOOKS, including its two imprints, Skipstone and Braided River, is a leading publisher of quality outdoor recreation, sustainability, and conservation titles. As a 501(c)(3) nonprofit, we are committed to supporting the environmental and educational goals of our organization by providing expert information on human-powered adventure, sustainable practices at home and on the trail, and preservation of wilderness.

Our publications are made possible through the generosity of donors, and through sales of 700 titles on outdoor recreation, sustainable lifestyle, and conservation. To donate, purchase books, or learn more, visit us online:

MOUNTAINEERS BOOKS
1001 SW Klickitat Way, Suite 201 • Seattle, WA 98134
800-553-4453 • mbooks@mountaineersbooks.org • mountaineersbooks.org

An independent nonprofit publisher since 1960

YOU MAY ALSO ENJOY: